It's a Win-When

Balancing Immediate Wins With Long-term Success, Making Great Decisions

By Kurt Peeplez

I0168087

It's a Win-When

It's a Win-When

Balancing Immediate Wins With Long-term Success, Making Great Decisions

By Kurt Peeplez

99th Ave Publishing
Phoenix, AZ U.S.A.

kurt@kpexec.com
kpexec.com
kurtrp.com

It's a Win-When

Published by:

99th Ave Publishing
Phoenix, AZ U.S.A.

kurtrp.com
kpexec.com

Copyright © 2024 by Kurt Peeplez
ISBN Paperback: 978-0-9771195-8-5
ASIN Kindle: B0DL6KCJGJ

Unattributed quotations are by Kurt Peeplez

Printed in the United States of America

IT'S A
WIN-WHEN

Balancing Immediate Wins With Long-term Success

MAKING GREAT DECISIONS

KURT PEEPLEZ

Table of Contents

About the Author

Kurt Peeplez is an author, seasoned business coach and entrepreneur. Armed with his passion for empowering business owners and his love of seeing people succeed, Kurt has spent years providing guidance and support to his community. As a youth sports coach, he is dedicated to inspiring the next generation to overcome obstacles, embrace their full potential, and achieve new heights of personal success. He has also authored several books on self-development and hopes to motivate his readers to seize control of their future goals and happiness.

In his professional career, Kurt strives to work together with business owners to realize their goals and objectives. He has served as a trusted partner and advisor to dozens of organizations, offering reliable guidance and solutions to a diverse range of business challenges. For more information, or to book his consulting services, visit his websites at www.kpexec.com or www.kurtrp.com

Foreword

In a world filled with choices, decisions, and consequences, "It's a Win When" presents a powerful guide to making decisions that not only benefit your present but also pave the way to a brighter future.

"The decisions you make today will shape the life you'll lead tomorrow."

Whether you're grappling with personal decisions, career moves, or life changes, the need for choices that serve both your present and future is universal.

Like you, I've faced moments where my decisions felt right at the time but led to unexpected regret, or where painful sacrifices eventually paved the way to long-term success. These experiences taught me that the art of decision-making is more than just making a choice, it's about making the right choice, one that allows you to thrive both now and in the future.

This book is designed to give you exactly that: a roadmap for making decisions that reward you today and set you up for tomorrow. Through the Win-When approach, you'll learn how to avoid the tension between short-term gratification and long-term success, and instead make choices that offer both. You'll gain the tools to:

It will take you through a step-by-step process for making decisions that lead to what I call "immediate and sustained wins." You'll reflect on past choices, uncover valuable lessons, and transform the way you approach decisions in the future.

By the end, you'll have a decision-making foundation that allows you to live with greater fulfillment, knowing that your choices are creating value today and setting you up for ongoing success.

As you read, you'll find that this isn't just another book about decision-making, it's a guide to reshaping the way you think about your life's direction. Each chapter offers practical strategies and reflections that empower you to take control of your future, one decision at a time.

Here's to making choices that allow you to thrive now and in the future. Let's begin the journey.

A Journey of Reflection

"The decisions you make today will shape the life you'll lead tomorrow."

As I look back over the years, I can remember some of the decisions I've made, some that seemed right at that moment in time, but didn't serve me well in the future, and others that paid off in the future but felt painful in the present. From starting and ending relationships to taking out unnecessary loans, choosing the wrong job opportunity, or even giving up too soon on a business venture, each decision shaped the course of my life in ways I didn't always expect.

I can recall the times I stayed quiet when I should've spoken up, when I acted on impulse instead of calming down, letting my emotion guide me, or when I didn't ask for advice even though I needed it. I often wished my decisions could benefit me both now and, in the future, because isn't that what we all want? Is that possible? We want to make choices that serve us in the present while setting us up for future success, right?

Take a moment to reflect on your own life. Think about the good and bad decisions

12

you've made and how they affected you. What were they based on? Emotion? Logic? Pressure? Did those decisions benefit you both in the present and the future? Or did it only benefit now or only later.

Think about those moments when you had to wait for the benefits of a decision to materialize. How did it feel to endure that long, uncertain stretch of time, wondering if your sacrifice would pay off?

In the wake of those decisions, how did it feel to have to endure until the benefits, the good part, kicked in? How did you feel enjoying the present reward, knowing that it would be short-lived, only temporary, because that decision wasn't going to benefit you in the long run.

Consider a decision to sacrifice time with your family for the sake of career advancement. You tell yourself it's for the greater good that by putting in extra hours at work at the present, you're securing a better future for your loved ones. But as you sit at your desk late at night or travel for business, missing another family dinner or your child's soccer game, you feel the strain on your relationships.

If you don't consider everything and seek input, it's possible that your children will grow up, your spouse becomes more distant, and though you may eventually enjoy the financial rewards of a promotion, you can't help but wonder if it was worth the cost. The long-term benefit comes at the expense of the present moments that can't be replaced, and the emotional distance that develops may leave a lasting impact on those closest to you.

The weight of choosing the future over the present can feel heavy, even agonizing. You knew the benefits would come, but waiting, the strain of holding on, can feel unbearable.

And what about those choices where you indulged in the moment, knowing full well that the reward was fleeting?

Taking out a loan to invest in a business or to cover a current need can feel like a smart, future-oriented decision until an emergency arises. That loan, which once seemed like a way to secure future growth, now leaves you without a safety net when you need it most. The immediate cost is felt in the lack of financial flexibility, and though the business or investment may thrive in the long run, the stress of not having a cushion for unexpected expenses takes its toll on your well-being and security. You're left enduring the pressure of tight cash flow, hoping that the future payoff will be worth the current strain.

The satisfaction fades quickly, leaving you with the sobering realization that the future is still waiting, unchanged and possibly even burdened by your short-term decision.

These moments of tension between present gratification and future benefit are crossroads we all face. It's not easy to balance, and sometimes the choices we make feel right but end up leaving us with regret.

The Win-When approach is here to change that. It's about making decisions that reward you now and in the future. These are decisions that won't make you choose between enjoying today or securing tomorrow, because it is possible for you to have both.

What if there was a decision-making foundation that would allow you to make choices that not only benefit you today but also lead to a better tomorrow? In this book, you'll learn how to do just that. We'll explore the mistakes you've made, and more importantly, how to start making better decisions, decisions that lead to immediate wins and long-term success, what I call the Win-When approach.

At its core, decision-making isn't just about choosing one path over another; it's about cutting off distractions, doubts, and conflicting directions that pull you away from your goals. We'll also help you avoid sacrifices that hurt more than they help.

The word "decide" comes from the Latin word "decidere," meaning "to cut off." Every meaningful decision is an act of eliminating other possibilities. When you decide to move forward in one direction, you're choosing to cut off paths that may have kept you in uncertainty or led you to an unproductive or unfavorable place.

In life, we often find ourselves at a crossroads with countless options, making it critical to decide on the right path. Every decision you make is an act of courage. It's a deliberate move to focus on a single possibility. Throughout this book, we'll delve into how making decisions with clarity and purpose is the key to achieving both immediate wins and lasting success.

A true win isn't just about getting the desired outcome. It's about making good decisions that reflect who you are and where you want to go. It's about cutting off the paths that no longer serve you and embracing the ones that do. Whether it's deciding on a career move, ending a relationship, or navigating a business challenge, each decision is a steppingstone toward a better future.

Win-Win vs. Win-When

The Win-Win philosophy, familiar to many, revolves around creating a situation where both parties benefit. It's about ensuring mutual gain, a valuable and widely used strategy in business and negotiation. However, the Win-Win approach doesn't specify when the benefit must occur. One party might gain immediately, while the other might see their return in the distant future. It's about compromise and balance, but it lacks the guarantee of immediate and ongoing benefits for each party involved.

This is where the Win-When concept adds an essential dimension. The Win-When approach focuses on making sure the decision doesn't just provide value at some indefinite point in time but delivers wins for you both now and in the future. It ensures that every choice you make creates an immediate benefit that is carried forward, impacting your future success as well. The emphasis is on continuity, making sure that the decision enhances your present and builds a foundation for future wins.

The Business Deal Example

Imagine negotiating a business deal. In a traditional Win-Win scenario, you might agree to terms that benefit you today, like receiving a lump sum payment upfront, while the other party benefits later through long-term access to your resources or services. You sold the business, got the cash, and you part friends. This can work, but it doesn't necessarily secure your future.

In contrast, under a Win-When philosophy, you would structure the deal to ensure that not only do you gain immediate financial benefit, but you also secure ongoing royalties or residuals that will continue to support you in the years to come. The Win-When concept ensures that your decision brings value both today and, in the future, guaranteeing sustained benefits.

The Career Move Example

Consider a career move. A Win-Win decision might involve taking a high-paying job now that offers immediate financial security but lacks room for growth or future advancement. On the other hand, the company benefits from your skills in the short term. However, under the Win-When approach, you would seek out a job that not only pays well now but also offers opportunities for future promotions, personal development, and career growth. In this way, your decision benefits both your present and your future, creating a more comprehensive and sustainable win.

The Win-When concept is powerful because it challenges you to think beyond the short-term and consider the broader impact of your decisions on both your present and future. It encourages you to assess how each choice you make today influences not just immediate outcomes, but also shapes your future trajectory. This strategic mindset fosters long-term planning, ensuring that your actions benefit you now while building a solid foundation for future success.

By embracing Win-When, you shift your focus from solving short-term problems to creating lasting, sustainable growth. It's about making decisions that open doors now and leave them open for future opportunities. This approach ensures that your present and future selves are equally served, balancing immediate gratification with long-term rewards.

This book will help you identify common pitfalls in decision-making and provide tools to avoid them, empowering you to consistently make choices that bring value in both the short and long term. By balancing the present with the future, and aligning your decisions with your core values, you'll begin to see a transformation in how you approach life.

So, let's begin the journey to building the foundation of good decisions, where both your present and future self will thank you.

Lessons From the Past

*"The eyes are useless when the mind is blind.
We must learn from the mistakes of our past."*

In the previous chapter, we explored the foundational importance of making good decisions. We introduced the Win-When concept as a framework for ensuring that the choices we make today set the stage for ongoing success and fulfillment. However, to truly appreciate the value of good decision-making, it's essential to understand the consequences of poor decisions.

History provides us with countless examples of decisions that, in hindsight, were clearly misguided. These examples are not just stories of failure; they are valuable lessons that illustrate the dangers of short-term thinking, emotional impulses, and a lack of foresight.

We will delve into the history of bad decisions, examining both personal and public life examples to uncover the common factors that lead to poor outcomes. By studying these examples, we can better understand the pitfalls to avoid in our own decision-making processes. The goal is to learn from the past so that we can make more informed, thoughtful, and ultimately successful decisions in the future.

One of the most common reasons people make bad decisions is short-term thinking. This occurs when individuals focus solely on immediate gratification or relief without considering the long-term consequences of their actions. While the allure of instant results can be powerful, the fallout from such decisions often leaves lasting damage.

A contemporary example of the perils of short-term thinking is the collapse of Enron in the early 2000s. Enron, once a darling of Wall Street, was an energy company that engaged in widespread accounting fraud to inflate its profits and stock price. The executives at Enron were focused on short-term gains, driven by greed and the desire to keep stock prices high.

However, this house of cards came crashing down when fraud was exposed, leading to one of the largest corporate bankruptcies in history. The fallout included the loss of thousands of jobs, billions of dollars in shareholder value, and a significant loss of trust in corporate governance. Enron's downfall serves as a stark reminder of how short-term thinking, driven by immediate financial gains, can lead to catastrophic consequences.

Another major contributor to bad decisions is emotional impulse. When emotions such as fear, anger, or excitement take the lead, rational thinking often takes a backseat. Decisions made in the heat of the moment are rarely well-considered and can lead to regret and negative outcomes.

One of the most famous examples of a disastrous decision made under the influence of emotions is the story of the Trojan Horse from Greek mythology. The Greeks, after failing to breach the walls of Troy for ten years, devised a cunning plan: they built a massive wooden horse, hid soldiers inside it, and left it outside the gates of Troy as an offering.

The Trojans, believing that their long siege was over and eager to celebrate their victory, allowed the horse into the city. That night, the Greek soldiers emerged from the horse and opened the gates for the rest of the Greek army, leading to the fall of Troy. The Trojans' decision to bring the horse inside was driven by the emotional desire to celebrate and believe in their victory, blinding them to the potential danger.

A modern example of the dangers of emotional decision-making is the Challenger Space Shuttle disaster in 1986. The decision to launch the shuttle, despite concerns from engineers about the safety of the O-ring seals in cold temperatures, was influenced by external pressures and the desire to maintain the launch schedule. The decision-makers were swayed by the emotional weight of public expectations and the desire to avoid delays, leading to a catastrophic failure that resulted in the loss of seven lives.

This tragedy highlights the risks of allowing emotions, such as the fear of public criticism or the desire to meet deadlines, to override logical and safety-based decision-making. It serves as a reminder that emotional impulses, when left unchecked, can lead to irreversible outcomes.

Another common factor in bad decision-making is the failure to consider potential consequences. This often happens when individuals or organizations focus on the immediate benefits without fully evaluating the risks and downsides.

In 1961, the United States launched the Bay of Pigs invasion, a failed military operation aimed at overthrowing the Cuban government of Fidel Castro. The plan was poorly conceived and based on the assumption that the Cuban people would revolt against Castro, which did not happen. The invasion was a disaster, leading to a significant loss of life, the capture of American forces, and a major diplomatic embarrassment for the U.S.

One of the key reasons for the failure was that the planners did not fully consider the potential consequences of the invasion. They underestimated Castro's support within Cuba and overestimated the likelihood of a popular uprising. The decision to proceed with the invasion, despite these uncertainties, was a classic example of ignoring potential consequences in favor of a hoped-for outcome.

External pressure, whether from peers, superiors, or societal expectations, can all lead to bad decisions. When individuals feel compelled to conform or act quickly due to external demands, they may make choices that they would otherwise avoid if given the time and space to think critically.

The Salem witch trials of 1692 are a chilling example of how external pressure can lead to terrible decisions. In a climate of fear and suspicion, accusations of witchcraft spread rapidly through the community of Salem, Massachusetts. Under pressure to act, local authorities conducted trials that led to the execution of 20 people and the imprisonment of many others.

The decision to prosecute and execute individuals based on flimsy evidence was driven by the external pressure of public fear and the desire to restore order. In the aftermath, many of those involved expressed regret and acknowledged the injustice of their actions. The Salem witch trials serve as a powerful reminder of how external pressure can lead to decisions that cause harm and leave lasting scars on a community.

Immediate gratification is another major factor in bad decision-making. The desire for instant rewards can cloud judgment and lead to choices that are detrimental in the long run.

In the early 2000s, Blockbuster was the dominant video rental company, with thousands of stores across the United States. However, as the digital age dawned and streaming services like Netflix began to emerge, Blockbuster faced a critical decision; adapt to the changing landscape or continue with its traditional business model.

The company chose the latter, prioritizing immediate profits from late fees and physical rentals over investing in digital streaming. This decision, driven by the desire for immediate gratification, ultimately led to Blockbuster's downfall. As consumers shifted to digital streaming, Blockbuster was left behind, and by 2010, the company filed for bankruptcy.

Blockbuster's failure to adapt serves as a cautionary tale about the dangers of clinging to short-term gains at the expense of long-term innovation and sustainability.

As you can see, the consequences of poor decisions can be devastating. The historical examples discussed here highlight the far-reaching consequences of poor decisions. Whether driven by short-term thinking, emotional impulses, external pressure, or the lure of immediate gratification, bad decisions can lead to a cascade of negative outcomes that affect individuals, organizations, and even entire societies.

Many bad decisions result in significant financial losses. Whether it's the collapse of a company, the loss of personal savings, or a broader economic crisis, the financial impact of poor choices can be devastating.

Bad decisions can also lead to a loss of trust and damage to one's reputation. This can be particularly harmful in professional settings, where reputation is a key asset. Once trust is broken, it can be challenging to rebuild, and the consequences can last for years.

The emotional and psychological toll of bad decisions should not be underestimated. Guilt, regret, and stress are common outcomes of poor choices, and these feelings can have long-lasting effects on mental health and well-being.

Poor decisions can also strain or even destroy relationships. Whether it's a decision that affects a family, a friendship, or a professional partnership, the fallout from a bad choice can create lasting rifts that are difficult to mend.

Finally, bad decisions often result in missed opportunities. When we make poor choices, we may close doors to future possibilities that could have led to growth, success, and fulfillment.

So why do we keep making bad decisions? Given the clear negative consequences of poor decision making, one might wonder why people continue to make them. The answer lies in the complex interplay of various factors, including cognitive biases, emotional states, social influences, and the inherent uncertainty of life.

One reason is human beings are prone to cognitive biases that can distort our thinking and lead to poor decisions. For example, the "confirmation bias" leads us to seek out information that confirms our existing beliefs, while the "status quo bias" causes us to prefer the familiar over the unknown, even if change would be beneficial.

Emotions also play a significant role. When we are stressed, angry, or fearful, our ability to think clearly and rationally is compromised. Emotional decision-making often leads to choices that prioritize immediate relief over long-term benefits.

The opinions and behaviors of others can heavily influence our decisions. Peer pressure, cultural norms, and societal expectations can lead us to make choices that align with the group, even if they conflict with our own best interests. This often results in us not being true to ourselves.

And let's not forget that life is inherently uncertain, and the fear of making the wrong choice can lead to indecision or a hasty decision. The need to manage risk and uncertainty is a significant challenge in decision-making, and it requires careful consideration and a willingness to embrace the unknown.

So, what do we do? While it's impossible to avoid all bad decisions, we can learn from the past and use that knowledge to make better choices in the future. The historical examples discussed in this chapter offer valuable lessons in the dangers of short-term thinking, emotional impulses, external pressure, and the pursuit of immediate gratification.

By understanding these factors, we will be able to recognize when we are at risk of making a poor choice and understand the steps to take to mitigate those risks. This might involve slowing down the decision-making process, seeking input from trusted advisors, or taking a step back to evaluate the long-term consequences of our actions.

Now that we've explored the factors that contribute to bad decisions, it's time to shift our focus to what makes a decision good.

In the next chapter, we will identify the signs of good decisions and how they contribute to both present and future success. By understanding the characteristics of good decision-making, we can develop strategies to consistently make choices that lead to positive outcomes in our present and in our future lives.

How To Recognize a Good Decision

*"A wise decision is a bridge
to a better tomorrow."*

So far, we have explored the pitfalls of bad decisions, examining how short-term thinking, emotional impulses, external pressures, and the lure of immediate gratification can lead to unfavorable outcomes. Understanding the consequences of poor decision-making is crucial, but equally important is the ability to recognize and cultivate the traits of making good decisions.

Good decisions have a certain resilience. They can withstand the test of time, providing benefits that extend beyond the immediate moment. They not only solve the problem at hand but also lay the groundwork for future success and fulfillment. In this chapter, we will delve into the key indicators that define good decision-making. By understanding these indicators, you will be better equipped to make choices that are not only wise in the present but also beneficial in the long term.

At its core, a good decision is one that aligns with your values, meets your immediate needs, and supports your long-term objectives. But what exactly makes a good decision "good"? Several key factors contribute to this.

A good decision is an informed choice and is rooted in solid, accurate, and comprehensive information. When faced with a decision, it's essential to gather as much relevant data as possible. This includes understanding the situation fully, considering all possible options, and evaluating the potential outcomes.

For instance, if you're considering a major career move, you would need to research the new industry, understand the job market, evaluate your skills against the job requirements, and consider the impact on your personal life. The more informed you are, with accurate data points, the better equipped you will be to make a decision that aligns with both your present and future needs.

It's important to note that being informed doesn't just mean having access to data; it also means understanding how to interpret that data. Critical thinking is crucial here, being able to discern which information is relevant, trustworthy, and significant to your decision-making process.

Rarely made in haste, good decisions require thoughtful deliberation and consideration. This means taking the time to weigh the pros and cons, considering the potential risks and rewards, and reflecting on how this decision aligns with your broader life goals.

Deliberation involves asking yourself these key questions:

- How will this decision impact me today?

- What are the potential long-term consequences?

- Does this choice align with my values and goals?

- What are the possible risks, and how can they be mitigated?

By thinking through these questions, you will ensure that your decision is not only practical and effective in the short term but also beneficial to you in the long run.

A good decision is one that is in harmony with your personal values and long-term objectives. Your values serve as a compass, guiding you toward choices that resonate with who you are and what you stand for. This is you being true to yourself. When a decision aligns with your values, it feels right at a deep, intuitive level, in your soul, even if it's challenging or requires sacrifice.

For example, if one of your core values is integrity, making a decision that involves deceit or cutting corners would likely lead to internal conflict and regret, even if it results in short-term gains. On the other hand, a decision that upholds your values will not only feel more satisfying but will also contribute to your long-term sense of fulfillment and purpose.

We've talked about short-term, but a good decision should also support your long-term objectives. Whether these objectives relate to your career, personal growth, relationships, or financial security, a decision that moves you closer to these goals is likely to be a good one.

One of the hallmarks of a good decision is its resilience, the ability of the decision to adapt to changing circumstances while still delivering positive outcomes. Life is unpredictable, and even the best-laid plans can be disrupted by unforeseen events. A resilient decision is one that can withstand these changes and continue to serve your best interests.

Decision resilience allows for adjustments as new information becomes available or as circumstances change. For example, if you decide to pursue further education while working, a resilient decision will include a plan for how to manage your time if your workload increases unexpectedly.

Good decision-makers think ahead and consider what might happen if things don't go as planned. They develop contingency plans to address potential challenges, ensuring that they can pivot quickly if needed. These kinds of decisions are not static; they are revisited and evaluated over time to ensure they are still serving your goals. This would involve checking in periodically to assess whether the decision is yielding the expected results or if adjustments are needed.

By building resilience in your choices, you increase the likelihood that they will continue to benefit you in the face of change and uncertainty. Good decisions strike a balance between addressing immediate needs and ensuring long-term success. This is the essence of the Win-When concept, making choices that provide a win now while also setting the stage for victories in the future.

Here's another example. Investing in a professional development course might require significant time commitment and upfront cost, but the long-term benefits, such as career advancement and increased earning potential, can far outweigh the initial investment.

While logic and reason are essential components of good decision-making, intuition also plays a crucial role. Your gut feelings are often informed by your subconscious mind, which has absorbed patterns and experiences over time. When faced with a decision, your intuition can provide valuable insights that might not be immediately apparent through logical analysis alone.

However, it's important to distinguish between intuition and impulsive reactions. Intuition is a deeper, more reflective sense of what feels right, whereas impulsive decisions are often driven by immediate emotions. By combining intuition with critical thinking, you can make decisions that are both rational and aligned with your deeper instincts.

These kinds of decisions are intertwined with personal growth. They are not only about achieving specific outcomes, but they also contribute to your personal growth and development. Every decision you make provides an opportunity to learn more about yourself, refine your values, and develop new skills and abilities.

When making a difficult decision, such as leaving a stable job to pursue a passion, you could be challenged to step out of your comfort zone and develop resilience, adaptability, and problem-solving skills. Even if the outcome is not exactly as you envisioned, the process of making and executing the decision can lead to significant personal growth and better decision-making over time.

Good decision making often involves taking responsibility for your choices and learning from the results. This sense of ownership is empowering and reinforces your ability to shape your own life. It also builds confidence in your decision-making abilities, which in turn helps you make better decisions in the future.

To further illustrate the characteristics of good decision-making, let's explore a few real-world case studies where individuals or organizations made decisions that not only solved immediate problems but also paved the way for long-term success.

Apple's Decision to Focus on Design and Innovation

In the late 1990s, Apple was struggling. The company had lost its edge in the personal computing market, and its product lineup was unfocused and unappealing. When Steve Jobs returned to Apple in 1997, he made a series of decisions that would ultimately transform the company into one of the most successful and innovative brands in the world.

Jobs' key decision was to focus on design and innovation, prioritizing a few high-quality products over a broad range of mediocre ones. This decision was informed by a deep understanding of the market, a clear vision for the company's future, and a commitment to Apple's core values of creativity and excellence.

The immediate benefit of this decision was a streamlined product lineup that resonated with consumers. The long-term impact was even more profound. Apple went on to revolutionize multiple industries with products like the iPod, iPhone, and iPad. Jobs' decision to focus on design and innovation not only saved Apple from potential bankruptcy but also positioned the company to sustain success in the future.

Cultivate the Habit of Good Decision-Making

Making good decisions is a skill that can be cultivated and refined over time. Here are some strategies to help you develop the habit of making sound decisions.

- Regularly reflect on your values, goals, and past decisions. This will help you develop a deeper understanding of what's important to you and how to align your decisions with your long-term objectives.

- When faced with a decision, seek input from others who have different perspectives and experiences. This can help you see the situation from multiple angles and avoid blind spots.

- Avoid making decisions in haste. Give yourself the time and space to consider all the relevant information and to think through the potential consequences.

- Review the outcomes of your past decisions, both good and bad. What worked? What didn't? Use these insights to improve your decision-making process in the future.

- While it's important to base your decisions on logic and reason, don't ignore your intuition. Your gut feelings can provide valuable insights that complement your analytical thinking.

- Be open to adjusting your decisions as circumstances change. A good decision is one that can adapt to new information and evolving situations.

Most importantly, view each decision as an opportunity to learn and grow. Over time, this commitment to continuous improvement will enhance your ability to make good decisions that lead to sustained success.

Now that we've identified the traits of good decisions, the next step is understanding how to consistently make them.

In the next chapter, we will introduce a structured process for decision-making that can help you make the right choices time and again. This process will guide you through each stage of decision-making, from gathering information to evaluating outcomes, ensuring that your decisions are informed, deliberate, and aligned with your values and goals.

The Process

"Don't make decisions when you're angry. Don't make promises when you're happy. And don't make plans when you're drunk."

We've explored the signs of good decisions, emphasizing the importance of making choices that are informed, deliberate, and aligned with both immediate and long-term goals. We also discussed the need for decisions to be resilient, capable of adapting to changing circumstances while continuing to deliver positive outcomes. But making good decisions consistently is not just a matter of luck or relying on intuition; it requires a structured approach.

In this chapter, we will introduce a step-by-step guide to the decision-making process. This process is designed to help you navigate the complexities of decision-making with confidence, ensuring that your choices are sound and aligned with your present needs and future aspirations. By following this process, you can increase the likelihood of making decisions that lead to sustained success and fulfillment.

This is a skill that can be developed and refined through practice. By following a structured process, you can approach each decision with clarity and purpose, reducing the risk of being swayed by short-term desires or external pressures. Below is a detailed breakdown of each step in the decision-making process:

Step 1: Define the Decision

The first and most crucial step in the decision-making process is to clearly define what decision needs to be made and the problem it aims to solve. This may seem straightforward, but it's often where people go wrong. Without a clear understanding of what the decision is, you risk making a choice that addresses the wrong issue or that only partially solves the problem.

Key Questions to Ask:

- What is the specific decision I need to make?

- What problem or opportunity am I addressing with this decision?

- What are the desired outcomes?

- Are there any underlying issues that need to be addressed first?

Imagine you are considering whether to take a new job offer. At first glance, the decision might seem to be simply about whether to accept the offer or not. However, by defining the decision more clearly, you might realize that the underlying issue is your desire for greater career growth, better work-life balance, or increased financial security. By understanding the true nature of the decision, you can better assess how the new job offer aligns with these goals.

Common Pitfalls:

- Failing to identify the real issue behind the decision.

- Defining the decision too broadly or too narrowly.

- Allowing external pressures to shape the decision before fully understanding it.

By taking the time to define the decision clearly, you lay the groundwork for making a choice that truly addresses your needs and objectives.

Step 2: Gather Information

Once you've determined what the decision is, the next step is to gather all relevant information. This involves collecting data, seeking out different perspectives, and understanding the context in which the decision will be made. The goal is to ensure that you have a comprehensive view of the situation before moving forward.

Key Questions to Ask:

- What information do I need to make an informed decision?

- Where can I find reliable data or insights?

- Who can provide valuable perspectives or expertise?

- What are the potential biases in the information I'm gathering?

Example: Continuing with the job offer scenario, gathering information might involve researching the company's culture, financial stability, and growth prospects. You might also seek input from current or former employees, consider the impact of the job on your family life, and assess the job market in your field.

Common Pitfalls:

- Relying on incomplete or outdated information.

- Ignoring or dismissing information that contradicts your initial inclinations.

- Failing to consider multiple perspectives or sources.

Effective decision-making requires a thorough understanding of the situation. By gathering comprehensive and accurate information, you increase the likelihood of making a well-informed choice.

Step 3: Weigh the Options

With the information in hand, the next step is to weigh the options. This involves considering the potential outcomes of each option, both positive and negative. It's important to think critically about the short-term and long-term consequences of each choice, as well as the risks and rewards.

Key Questions to Ask:

- What are the possible options available to me?

- What are the potential benefits and drawbacks of each option?

- How does each option align with my values and goals?

- What are the short-term and long-term consequences of each option?

Example: In the job offer scenario, weighing the options might involve considering the benefits of taking the new job (higher salary, career advancement) against the potential drawbacks (longer commute, travel, higher stress). You might also consider alternative options, such as negotiating the terms of the offer or staying in your current position.

Common Pitfalls:

- Focusing too much on the immediate benefits while overlooking long-term consequences.

- Underestimating the risks associated with certain options.

- Allowing emotions to cloud your judgment.

By carefully weighing the options, you can identify the choice that offers the best balance of benefits and risks, both now and in the future.

Step 4: Align with Values and Goals

A critical aspect of good decision-making is ensuring that your choice aligns with your core values and long-term objectives. This step involves reflecting on what truly matters to you and considering how each option fits into your broader life plan.

Key Questions to Ask:

- Does this decision align with my core values?

- How does this choice support my long-term goals?

- Will this decision bring me closer to the life I want to create?

- Are there any potential conflicts between this decision and my values or goals?

Example: If one of your core values is work-life balance, you might consider how the new job offer aligns with this value. Does the job offer flexible working conditions? Will the increased salary come at the cost of spending less time with your family? By reflecting on these questions, you can make a decision that not only meets your immediate needs but also supports your long-term well-being.

Common Pitfalls:

- Compromise your values for short-term gains.

- Losing sight of your long-term goals in the face of immediate pressures.

- Making decisions based on external validation rather than internal alignment.

Aligning your decisions with your values and goals ensures that the choices you make contribute to a life that is meaningful and fulfilling.

Step 5: Make the Decision

After gathering information, weighing up the options, and ensuring alignment with your values and goals, it's time to make the decision. This is the moment when you choose the option that you believe offers the best balance between immediate and future benefits.

Key Questions to Ask:

- Am I confident that I've considered all relevant factors?

- Does this decision feel right, both logically and intuitively?

- What is the best way to communicate and implement this decision?

- How can I prepare for any potential challenges that may arise?

Example: If, after careful consideration, you decide to accept the new job offer, you might begin by negotiating the terms to better align with your values and goals. Your communication skills will be invaluable in this, setting the tone for understanding, cooperation and acceptance of what you have decided. You should also start planning for the transition, considering how to manage the change effectively.

Common Pitfalls:

- Overthinking and delaying the decision.

- Allowing fear of making the wrong choice paralyzes you.

- Deciding impulsively without fully considering the consequences.

- Saying things the wrong way, clouding the matter, and causing confusion or misunderstandings.

Making a decision is an act of commitment. Once you've made your choice, it's important to move forward confidently with a plan for implementation.

Step 6: Evaluate and Adjust

The final step in the decision-making process is to evaluate the decision after it has been implemented. This involves assessing the impact of the decision and being willing to make adjustments if necessary. A good rule is to re-evaluate your goals and objectives every 90 days. No decision is set in stone, and being open to feedback and change is crucial for long-term success.

Key Questions to Ask:

- What has been the outcome of my decision so far?

- Are there any unintended consequences that need to be addressed?

- What can I learn from this decision-making process?

- Do I need to make any adjustments to improve the outcome?

Example: After accepting the new job, you might find that the role is more demanding than anticipated, affecting your work-life balance. In this case, you might need to adjust by setting clearer boundaries, seeking additional support, or even reconsidering your long-term career path.

Common Pitfalls:

- Failing to evaluate the decision and its outcomes.

- Being resistant to making necessary adjustments.

- Ignoring feedback or signs that the decision isn't working as intended.

Evaluating and adjusting your decisions ensures that you remain on the right path, even as circumstances change. It's an essential part of maintaining decision resilience and ensuring that your choices continue to serve your best interests.

By following this structured decision-making process, you can build greater confidence in your ability to make good decisions. This confidence comes from knowing that you have carefully considered all relevant factors, aligned your choices with your values and goals, and are prepared to adapt as needed.

It's important to remember that no decision-making process is foolproof. Even with the best intentions and careful planning, outcomes can be unpredictable. However, by approaching decisions with a clear process, you increase the likelihood of making choices that lead to positive outcomes.

Additionally, as you practice this process, you will become more attuned to your own decision-making patterns. You'll begin to recognize when you're falling into common pitfalls, such as rushing decisions, ignoring key information, or compromising your values. This self-awareness will help you refine your approach and make even better decisions in the future.

While the decision-making process outlined above is largely analytical, it's important to acknowledge the role of emotional intelligence in making good decisions. Emotional intelligence involves the ability to recognize, understand, and manage your own emotions, as well as the emotions of others.

Are you making a choice out of fear, anger, or excitement? Recognizing these emotions allows you to pause and ensure that your decision is based on sound reasoning rather than a temporary emotional state.

The ability to control your emotional impulses is key to making good decisions. This means resisting the urge to make hasty choices and instead taking the time to reflect and deliberate.

Also, considering the impact of your decisions on others is an important part of the process. Empathy allows you to see the situation from different perspectives and make choices that are considerate and inclusive.

Effective communication and relationship management are essential for implementing decisions, especially when they involve others.

By integrating emotional intelligence into your decision-making process, you will make choices that are not only logical but also emotionally balanced and considerate of the broader impact. Don't try to apply everything all at once. Do a little at a time. Don't take any shortcuts and you'll do great.

Now that you have a strong understanding of the decision-making process, the next step is to see how this process is applied in real-life scenarios. In the next several chapters, we will explore a variety of examples in both personal and business contexts, illustrating how the Win-When approach can be used to make decisions that benefit both your present and your future. These examples will provide practical insights into how you can apply the process to your own life, helping you make decisions that lead to sustained success and fulfillment.

Practical Application

*"One good example is worth
a thousand words of advice."*

In previous chapters, we built a foundation for understanding the importance of making good decisions. We began by exploring the profound impact that decisions have on our lives, both in the present and the future. We examined the traits of good decisions, highlighting how they align with our values and long-term goals while also being resilient to changing circumstances. We then outlined a structured decision-making process designed to help you consistently make choices that lead to sustained success and fulfillment.

However, while book knowledge is invaluable, the true power of the Win-When approach lies in its practical application. Understanding the principles of good decision-making is only the first step. The real challenge is putting those principles into action in your daily life. This chapter serves as a segway from theory to practice, setting the stage for the real-life scenarios that will be explored in the subsequent chapters.

These scenarios will demonstrate how the Win-When approach can be effectively applied to a wide range of situations, from personal relationships and career choices to financial decisions and business strategies. By analyzing these examples, you will gain practical insights into how to use the Win-When framework to navigate the complexities of decision-making in your own life.

Before diving into specific examples, it's important to recap the key concepts we've covered so far, as they will form the backbone of the analysis in the following scenarios. Each scenario will be structured around the principles and process outlined earlier, ensuring a consistent approach to decision-making.

We begin with the fundamental understanding from Chapter 1: that every decision we make shapes the trajectory of our lives, influencing not only our own happiness and success but also the well-being of those around us. The Win-When approach, which emphasizes balancing present and future outcomes, will be the lens through which each scenario is viewed. This approach ensures that the decisions made are not only beneficial at the immediate moment but also contribute to long-term success and fulfillment.

In Chapter 2, we explored the history of bad decisions, identifying common pitfalls such as short-term thinking, emotional impulses, and external pressures. By understanding these dangers, we can better recognize when we might be at risk of making a poor choice. The scenarios will highlight how these pitfalls are avoided by applying the Win-When approach, ensuring that decisions are made with careful consideration of both the immediate and long-term consequences.

Chapter 3 introduced the signs of good decisions, emphasizing the importance of making choices that are informed, deliberate, and aligned with our values and goals. These traits will be evident in each scenario, as we explore how the decision-makers gathered information, weighed their options, and ensured that their choices were consistent with their broader life objectives.

Finally, in Chapter 4, we outlined a structured decision-making process that provides a step-by-step guide to making good decisions consistently. The process of defining the decision, gathering information, weighing the options, aligning with values and goals, making the decision, and evaluating and adjusting will serve as the framework for analyzing each scenario. By following this process, the examples will demonstrate how to approach decision-making in a systematic and thoughtful way, increasing the likelihood of achieving positive outcomes both now and in the future.

One of the key elements that will be emphasized in the scenarios is the importance of communication in the decision-making process. Making a good decision is only part of the equation; how you communicate that decision is equally crucial. The way you express your choices can significantly influence how they are received by others and how effectively they are implemented.

Effective communication is about more than just conveying information, it's about ensuring that your message is understood, respected, and acted upon. This involves being clear, concise, and considerate in how you present your decision, as well as being open to constructive feedback and discussion. Whether you're communicating a decision to a colleague, a partner, or a broader audience, the way you frame your message can make all the difference in achieving the desired outcome.

In each scenario, we will explore how the decision-maker communicated their choice, considering factors such as the tone, timing, and context of the communication. We will also look at how they managed any potential conflicts or misunderstandings that arose, and how they ensured their decision was implemented effectively.

By focusing on communication, we recognize that decision-making does not happen in a silo or isolation. It involves interacting with others, exploring different perspectives, and managing expectations. Good communication is the bridge that connects the decision you make to the results you achieve, making it a vital component of the Win-When approach.

The following chapters will present a series of scenarios that illustrate how the Win-When approach can be applied in real-life situations. These scenarios will cover a diverse range of topics, from personal relationships and career decisions to financial planning and business strategy. Each scenario will be analyzed using the structured decision-making process, ensuring a consistent and comprehensive approach.

In each scenario, we will begin by defining the decision that needs to be made, identifying the problem or opportunity at hand. We will then examine how the decision-maker gathered information, considering the various factors that influenced their choice. Next, we will explore how they weighed their options, carefully considering the potential outcomes and aligning their choice with their values and long-term goals.

Once the decision is made, we will look at how it was communicated, emphasizing the importance of clear and effective communication in ensuring that the decision is understood and supported by others. Finally, we will evaluate the outcome, considering both the immediate and long-term benefits of the decision, and reflect on adjustments that were necessary along the way.

By analyzing these scenarios, you will see how the Win-When approach can be a powerful tool for navigating the complexities of decision-making in your own life. Whether you are facing a difficult personal decision, a challenging career choice, or a complex business problem, the principles and process we have discussed can help you make choices that lead to success both now and in the future.

These scenarios demonstrate the practical application of the Win-When approach, showing how theoretical concepts can be translated into real-world decisions. By seeing how others have applied these principles to their own lives, you will gain valuable insights into how to navigate your own decision-making challenges in your life.

The Win-When approach is not just about making good decisions. It's about being intentional in your choices, thoughtful in your process, and effective in your communication. As you move through the scenarios, you will see how this approach can transform your decision-making. This is your opportunity to learn, reflect, and refine your decision-making skills, helping you build a foundation for long-term success and fulfillment.

A New Job Offer

"If you don't ask, the answer isn't no."

Alyssa Walker sat at her small, wooden desk, the late afternoon sunlight streaming through the window of her cozy apartment. The soft click of her computer keyboard echoed into the otherwise quiet room as she reread the email that had just landed in her inbox. After months of searching, submitting resumes, and attending nerve-wracking interviews, she had finally received the email she had been hoping for, a job offer from Pinnacle Corp.

Pinnacle Corp was a tech giant, the kind of company that every software engineer dreamed of working for. The salary offered was significantly higher than what she was earning at her current job, enough to move out of her small apartment and into the downtown condo she had been eyeing. It also came with a benefits package that seemed too good to be true and the promise of rapid career advancement. The possibilities appeared endless.

But there was a catch.

60

Alyssa had heard some uncomfortable things about Pinnacle Corp, whispers among peers and online reviews that painted a picture of a demanding work culture. Stories of long hours, high pressure, and a competitive environment where employees were often pitted against each other were common. The rumors of burnout and a toxic atmosphere lingered in her mind as she stared at the offer, torn between excitement and apprehension.

She leaned back in her chair, closing her eyes and trying to quiet the storm of thoughts swirling in her head. On the one hand, this was the opportunity she had been working toward for years. The projects at Pinnacle were cutting-edge, and the prestige of working there would undoubtedly open doors for her in the future. On the other hand, she couldn't ignore the nagging doubt in her mind about the company's work environment. She had been in stressful jobs before, and the toll they took on her mental health was not something she was eager to visit again.

Her current job at Axis Innovations, a small start-up, was far from perfect. The work was uninspiring, the pay modest, and the opportunities for growth were limited. But the team was supportive, and the work-life balance allowed her to maintain her sanity. She had the time and energy to pursue her hobbies, stay connected with friends, and even volunteer on weekends. It wasn't the career she had envisioned for herself, but it was comfortable and stable.

The decision weighed heavily on her as she opened her eyes and gazed at the email again. Could she really thrive at Pinnacle Corp, or would she be stepping into a situation that would ultimately lead to burnout? She needed more information before she could make a good decision.

Step 1: Define the Decision

Alyssa knew that the first step in making a good decision was to clearly define what decision needed to be made. At first glance, the decision seemed simple: should she accept the job offer from Pinnacle Corp or stay at Axis Innovations? But as she thought about it more deeply, she realized there was more at stake. This wasn't just about taking a new job, it was about her long-term career goals, her mental health, and her overall happiness.

She asked herself the key questions she had learned from her study of the Win-When approach:

- What is the specific decision I need to make?
- What problem or opportunity am I addressing with this decision?

- What are the desired outcomes?
- Are there any underlying issues that need to be addressed first?

She realized that the underlying issue was her desire for greater career growth and financial security. The job at Pinnacle offered both, but at what cost? She wanted to advance her career, but not at the expense of her well-being. By clearly defining the decision, she understood that it wasn't just about the job offer; it was about aligning her career with her long-term goals and values.

Step 2: Gather Information

With the decision clearly defined, Alyssa knew the next step was to gather as much information as possible. She needed to understand Pinnacle Corp's work culture, the potential benefits and drawbacks of accepting the job, and how this decision would impact on her life both now and in the future.

She spent the next few days scouring the internet for information. She read anonymous employee reviews on Glassdoor, which ranged from glowing to scathing. Some employees praised the company's innovation and the chance to work on high-profile projects, while others warned of relentless pressure, lack of support from management, and a high turnover rate.

Alyssa also reached out to a former colleague, Sam, who had worked at Pinnacle for a couple of years before leaving. They met at a café one evening, where Sam shared his experience over a cup of coffee.

"It's true," Sam admitted, stirring his coffee slowly. "The projects are amazing, and the resources are unparalleled. But the culture... it's tough. You're expected to be available 24/7, and there's little room for error. They reward results, but if you slip up, you're out. It wore me down after a while."

Alyssa frowned, the knot in her stomach tightening. "But was there any room for negotiation? Could I set boundaries and still succeed there?"

Sam thought for a moment before replying. "Some people do manage to carve out a niche for themselves, but it's rare. You'd have to be very clear about your expectations from the start. But even then, it's a gamble. You might get what you want, or you might find yourself in over your head."

As they parted ways, Alyssa felt more conflicted than ever. The idea of working at Pinnacle was tempting, but she knew she needed more than just a big paycheck. She needed a job where she could thrive, not just survive.

Step 3: Weigh the Options

Armed with the information she had gathered; Alyssa began to weigh her options. She made a list of the potential benefits and drawbacks of accepting the job at Pinnacle Corp. The benefits were clear: a higher salary, career advancement, and the chance to work on exciting projects. But the drawbacks were just as significant: long hours, high stress, and the risk of burnout.

She also considered the option of staying at Axis Innovations. The benefits included a supportive work environment, a manageable workload, and a good work-life balance. But the drawbacks were equally clear: limited career growth, uninspiring work, and a lower salary.

As she weighed the options, Alyssa considered the following:

What are the possible options available to me?

- Should I accept the offer from Pinnacle Corp with the promise of a higher salary, career advancement, and prestigious projects, or should I remain at Axis Innovations where I have job security, work-life balance, and a supportive environment?

What are the potential benefits and drawbacks of each option?

- If I accept the job at Pinnacle Corp, will the benefits of career growth and financial security outweigh the risks of burnout and high-pressure culture?

- If I stay at Axis, will the comfort of work-life balance and supportive colleagues be worth the trade-off of limited career growth and lower pay?

How does each option align with my values and goals?

- Does the demanding environment at Pinnacle conflict with my value of maintaining mental health and work-life balance, even though it supports my long-term goal of career advancement and having financial stability?

- Does staying at Axis align more closely with my value of mental well-being, even though it falls short of my career and financial goals?

What are the short-term and long-term consequences of each option?

- In the short term, will accepting the Pinnacle offer provide immediate financial rewards but potentially strain my mental health?

- Will staying at Axis provide immediate comfort and stability but limit my long-term professional growth?

- Long-term, will the prestige and experience at Pinnacle open doors for future opportunities, or will I burn out before I can reap those benefits?

- Will staying at Axis give me continued peace of mind but cause stagnation in my career?

She realized that while the job at Pinnacle offered immediate benefits, the long-term consequences could be detrimental if she wasn't able to manage the demands of the role. On the other hand, staying at Axis Innovations would provide stability but at the cost of career growth and financial advancement.

Step 4: Align with Values and Goals

Alyssa knew that any decision she made had to align with her core values and long-term goals. She valued work-life balance, mental health, and meaningful work. She also had long-term goals of advancing in her career, achieving financial security, and finding a role that challenged and inspired her.

She reflected on how the job at Pinnacle Corp aligned with these values and goals. The higher salary would help her achieve financial security, and the challenging projects would provide the career growth she desired. However, the demanding work culture conflicted with the value of maintaining a healthy work-life balance.

She also thought about how staying at Axis Innovations aligned with her values and goals. The supportive environment allowed her to maintain her mental health and work-life balance, but the lack of career growth and financial advancement didn't align with her long-term goals.

After much reflection, Alyssa realized that while the job at Pinnacle Corp had the potential to fulfill her long-term goals, it would only do so if she could maintain her well-being in the process. She needed to find a way to align the job offer with her values, or it wouldn't be worth the risk.

Step 5: Make the Decision

After gathering information, weighing the options, and aligning the decision with her values and goals, it was time for Alyssa to make a decision. She knew that she couldn't be delayed any longer. The offer from Pinnacle Corp was too good to pass up, but only if she could ensure that it wouldn't come at the expense of her well-being.

The next morning, Alyssa took a deep breath and dialed the number of the hiring manager at Pinnacle Corp. Her heart pounded in her chest as she waited for the call to connect.

"Hello, Mr. Hartman," she began when the voice on the other end greeted her. "First of all, thank you for the offer. I'm genuinely excited about the possibility of joining Pinnacle Corp."

"I'm glad to hear that, Alyssa," Mr. Hartman replied. "We were very impressed with your interview and would love to have you on board."

"I appreciate that," Alyssa said, her voice steady. "However, before I accept, I would like to discuss how this role aligns with my long-term career goals and expectations for a positive work environment."

There was a brief pause at the other end of the line. "Of course," Mr. Hartman said. "What did you have in mind?"

Alyssa took another deep breath. "I want to ensure that the role allows for a healthy work-life balance. I've heard that Pinnacle can be very demanding, and while I'm eager to contribute, I also want to be clear that maintaining my well-being is a priority for me. I'm hoping we can discuss expectations around working hours, project deadlines, and the level of support available for employees."

Mr. Hartman's tone remained professional, but there was a hint of hesitation. "Pinnacle is a fast-paced environment, Alyssa, and we expect a lot from our employees. That being said, we're always open to discussing how we can support our team members. I can't promise anything out of the ordinary, but we can certainly work together to find a balance that works."

Alyssa nodded, even though he couldn't see her. "I understand. I'd also like to discuss opportunities for growth and how my role can evolve over time. I want to make sure that this position not only challenges me but also helps me build the skills and experience necessary for the next stage in my career."

Mr. Hartman's response was more encouraging this time. "That's something we can definitely discuss. We value employees who are looking to grow within the company, and there are plenty of opportunities for advancement at Pinnacle."

They spent the next thirty minutes hashing out details, with Alyssa pushing for as much clarity as possible. By the end of the conversation, she had a better understanding of what she could expect and where there might be room for compromise.

"Thank you for taking the time to discuss this with me," Alyssa said as they wrapped up. "I'll need a day or two to think it over, but I'm leaning toward accepting the offer."

"We'd be thrilled to have you," Mr. Hartman replied. "Let me know as soon as you've made your decision."

Step 6: Evaluate and Adjust

After the call, Alyssa spent the next day reflecting on the conversation. Pinnacle Corp was still a risk, but she felt more confident after discussing her concerns with Mr. Hartman. The company might not be perfect, but the opportunities it offered were undeniable. The question now was whether she was ready to take the leap, knowing that the work environment might still be challenging.

She made a list of pros and cons, weighing the potential for career growth against the possibility of burnout. She thought about her current job, where she felt safe but unfulfilled, and about the future she wanted to build for herself. She also considered the possibility that even if Pinnacle's culture was demanding, she could set boundaries and advocate for herself.

By the time the sun began to set, Alyssa had made up her mind. She would accept the offer, but only if Pinnacle agreed to the conditions they had discussed. She would enter the role with her eyes wide open, ready to work hard but also determined to protect her well-being.

The next morning, she called Mr. Hartman back.

"Good morning, Mr. Hartman," Alyssa began when he picked up. "After careful consideration, I've decided to accept the offer. However, I want to reiterate the importance of maintaining a healthy work-life balance and my commitment to both my personal growth and the company's success. I'm excited to join Pinnacle Corp and contribute to its innovative projects."

"We're excited to have you, Alyssa," Mr. Hartman replied. "I'm confident that you'll be a great addition to the team. Welcome aboard."

Alyssa smiled as she hung up the phone, feeling a mixture of excitement and nerves. She had taken a risk, but it was a calculated one. The future was uncertain, but she felt ready to face it, armed with the knowledge that she had made the best decision for herself, both now and in the long term.

Leveraging the Win-When Concepts

Alyssa's journey in deciding whether to accept the job at Pinnacle Corp is a clear illustration of the Win-When concepts. Faced with the immediate allure of a higher salary and prestigious role, she didn't rush into a decision based solely on present benefits. Instead, she carefully considered how the opportunity would impact both her current situation and her future well-being.

The Win-When approach emphasizes the importance of balancing present gains with long-term sustainability, and Alyssa exemplified this by negotiating for a positive work environment before committing to the role. She recognized the potential pitfalls of accepting a job with a questionable culture but also saw the possibility for significant career growth. By discussing her concerns openly with the hiring manager, she was able to set expectations that would support her both now and in the future.

Alyssa's decision-making process also highlighted the principle of personal accountability. She took charge of her career path, asking the right questions and setting boundaries that aligned with her long-term goals. Rather than being swayed by the immediate reward of a higher salary, she made a decision that would benefit her overall well-being and career development, even if it meant taking a risk.

In the end, Alyssa's story is one of empowerment and thoughtful decision-making. She didn't just aim for a "win" in the present but positioned herself for continued success in the future, embodying the essence of the Win-When philosophy.

If At First You Do Succeed

"Do not judge a man for where he is standing because you don't know how far he has come."

David Morrison sat at his kitchen table, the sunlight filtering through the window, casting a warm glow over the room. It was a quiet Saturday morning, and he was enjoying the peace that came with the weekend. At 57, David was a senior consultant at Apex Solutions, a man who had built a respected career over decades of hard work and determination. He had risen through the ranks without the benefit of a traditional degree, proving his worth through sheer grit and intelligence. The industry knew him as a strategic thinker, a problem solver, and someone who could be relied upon in even the toughest situations.

As he sipped his coffee, David's laptop chimed with the arrival of a new email. He opened it, his brow furrowing slightly as he read the message from the University of Pennsylvania. Over thirty years ago, David had been a student there, but he had left two years short of earning his degree. A lucrative job offer had drawn him away, and he had never looked back, until now. The email was offering him a chance to return to school and finish what he had started, part of a new program aimed at alumni who had left without completing their degrees.

David leaned back in his chair, letting out a thoughtful sigh. The idea of going back to school at his age seemed almost laughable. He was successful, nearing retirement, and had achieved more than many of his peers who had followed the traditional academic path. In five to seven years, he planned to retire, spend more time with his wife Susan, travel, and enjoy the fruits of his labor. So why did this email unsettle him?

He closed the laptop and pushed the thought away, focusing instead on the tasks of the day. But the idea lingered, refusing to be ignored. That evening, as he and Susan sat down for dinner, he brought it up.

"Hey, Susan," David began, cutting into his steak. "I got an email from Penn today. They're offering a program for people like me who never finished their degrees."

Susan looked up from her plate, her eyes curious. "Really? That's interesting. Are you thinking about it?"

David shrugged. "Not really. I mean, what's the point? I've done well without it, and I'm close to retirement. Going back to school now seems like a distraction."

Susan smiled softly, sensing his uncertainty. "True, but you always said you regretted not finishing your degree. Maybe this is your chance to close that chapter."

David swirled the wine in his glass, contemplating her words. "Maybe, but it feels like it would be more of a hassle than it's worth. I'm happy with where I am. Plus, going back to school at my age? I'd feel out of place."

Susan reached across the table and placed her hand over his. "You've never let fear hold you back before. But if you don't think it's worth it, that's okay too. Just make sure you're making the decision for the right reasons."

David nodded, appreciating her support. But the question lingered: Was it worth considering?

Step 1: Define the Decision

Over the next few days, David couldn't shake the thought of returning to school. It was an opportunity to finish something he had started long ago, a chance to tie up loose ends. But was that really what he wanted, or was he just entertaining an old regret?

David knew that before making any decision, he needed to clearly define what was at stake. The initial decision seemed straightforward: should he accept the offer to return to school or not? But as he delved deeper, he realized that the real issue was not about finishing a degree. It was about whether this step would add value to his life, both now and in the future.

He asked himself the key questions highlighted in the Win-When approach that had guided him through many tough decisions in the past:

- What is the specific decision I need to make?

- What problem or opportunity am I addressing with this decision?

- What are the desired outcomes?

- Are there any underlying issues that need to be addressed first?

David recognized that the underlying issue wasn't just about the degree. It was about his desire to finish something he had left incomplete, to achieve a sense of closure. But he also had to consider the broader implications, how would this impact on his current life and his plans for the future?

Step 2: Gather Information

David decided to gather more information to make an informed decision. He started by researching the program offered by the university. It was designed for working professionals, with flexible online classes and a curriculum tailored to adult learners. The program was manageable and wouldn't require him to take a leave of absence from his job. But it would still demand a significant time commitment.

He also considered his current situation. His consulting work was demanding, but he had built a routine that allowed him to maintain a good work-life balance. He was respected in his field, and his reputation had been built on decades of experience. Did he really need a degree to validate that?

David reached out to a few colleagues who had returned to school later in life. Their experiences were varied, some found it fulfilling, while others felt it was more of a burden than a benefit. One colleague, in particular, shared that going back to school had been a rewarding experience but had also added stress and taken time away from his family life.

This information gave David a clearer picture, but the decision was still not easy. He had to weigh the potential benefits against the drawbacks and consider how this choice aligned with his current priorities.

Step 3: Weigh the Options

With the information in hand, David began to weigh his options. On one side, there was the personal fulfillment of finally earning his degree, the satisfaction of finishing what he had started. It would also set an example for his children and grandchildren, showing them the value of lifelong learning and perseverance.

On the other hand, there was the reality of the time and effort it would take. Returning to school could mean less time with his family, more stress, and the possibility that it wouldn't make a significant difference in his professional life at this stage.

David also considered his plans for the future. He and Susan had been discussing retirement, traveling, and enjoying their golden years. Returning to school could delay these plans or add unnecessary stress during a time when he wanted to focus on other priorities.

As he weighed these options, David asked himself:

What are the specific opportunities available to me?

- Should I continue my career as is, content with the success I've achieved without a degree, or should I seize this chance to finish what I started decades ago by returning to school?

What are the personal and professional benefits and challenges of each option?

- If I go back to school, will it provide me with personal fulfillment and closure, or will it add unnecessary stress and take time away from my family and career?

- If I stay on my current path, am I missing out on an opportunity to set a lasting example for my family about the importance of education?

How does each option reflect my core values and long-term goals?

- Would returning to school align with my desire for balance and family time as I approach retirement, or would it contradict my commitment to enjoying the life I've worked hard to build?

- Is finishing the degree something I value today, or is it based on a past version of my goals?

What are the immediate and future impacts of each decision?

- Will going back to school now affect my work-life balance, delaying my retirement plans and taking time away from family?

- Alternatively, will earning the degree provide lasting benefits that align with my post-retirement goals, or will it prove less meaningful in the long run?

He realized that while finishing his degree might offer a sense of closure, it could also detract from the things he valued most, his family, his health, and his enjoyment of life. The degree was a goal he had once pursued, but it no longer seemed essential to his happiness or success.

Step 4: Align with Values and Goals

A critical aspect of David's decision-making process was ensuring that whatever choice he made aligned with his core values and long-term goals. He valued family, balance, and the satisfaction of knowing he had built a successful career through hard work and integrity.

David reflected on how returning to school fit into these values and goals. He considered whether earning the degree would bring him closer to the life he wanted to create or if it was simply a way to address an old regret.

One of David's core values was work-life balance. He had worked hard to achieve this balance, and he knew that returning to school would disrupt it. He also valued time with his family, especially as he neared retirement. Would pursuing this degree take away from the quality time he wanted to spend with Susan, his children, and his grandchildren?

By aligning the decision with his values and goals, David realized that while the degree was something he once wanted, it wasn't essential to his current or future happiness. It was a goal from a different time in his life, one that no longer held the same significance.

Step 5: Make the Decision

After gathering information, weighing the options, and reflecting on how this decision aligned with his values and goals, David knew it was time to make a decision. He didn't want to rush into it, but he also didn't want to overthink it and delay unnecessarily.

On a crisp Monday morning, David took a walk around his neighborhood. The quiet, tree-lined streets helped clear his mind as he considered his options. He thought about his career, the life he had built, and the future he wanted to enjoy with his family.

The degree, he realized, was something he had once pursued, but it wasn't essential to who he was today. He had already achieved success and fulfillment in his career and personal life. He didn't need a degree to validate that.

Returning home, David sat down at his desk and drafted an email to the university. He thanked them for the opportunity and expressed his appreciation, but he declined the offer to return to school. It wasn't the right time for him, and he knew his priorities lay elsewhere.

As he sent the email, David felt a sense of relief and clarity. He made the right decision, one that honored his past but focused on his future. He was ready to embrace the next chapter of his life without any lingering doubts.

Step 6: Evaluate and Adjust

In the weeks that followed, David occasionally thought about the decision he made about not pursuing the degree. He felt confident that he had chosen the path that best aligned with his values and goals. But he also knew that life was unpredictable and that he needed to remain open to reassessing his choices as circumstances changed.

David kept a close eye on his work-life balance, ensuring that he continued to prioritize the things that mattered most to him. He also made a point to revisit his goals regularly, reflecting on whether they still aligned with his vision for the future.

By evaluating and adjusting his decisions, David maintained a sense of direction and purpose in his life. He remained committed to making choices that would benefit him both now and, in the future, embodying the Win-When approach to his life.

Leveraging the Win-When Concepts

David's decision to decline the opportunity to return to school demonstrates a thoughtful application of the Win-When approach. At first glance, the idea of finishing his degree might have seemed like a win, a chance to complete something left unfinished and add another credential to his name. However, David wisely considered the broader impact of this decision on both his present and future.

The Win-When philosophy emphasizes balancing immediate desires with long-term well-being and success. David recognized that while returning to school could fulfill an old dream, it might also detract from his current priorities, spending time with his family and preparing for a fulfilling retirement. By choosing to focus on what truly mattered to him, David avoided the trap of pursuing a goal that would have added unnecessary stress and potentially taken away from the joy of his later years.

Furthermore, David's approach demonstrated personal accountability, another key tenet of the Win-When mindset. He sought advice from trusted sources, weighed his options carefully, and made a decision that aligned with his values and future plans. He didn't let external pressures or past regrets dictate his choice; instead, he took control of his narrative and chose the path that would bring him the most fulfillment in the long run.

In the end, David's story is a powerful reminder that not every opportunity needs to be pursued to achieve a "win." Sometimes, the best decision is to let go of what no longer serves us and focus on the goals and relationships that will bring true satisfaction and happiness, both now and in the future.

The Breaking Point

"It's not ok to set yourself on fire to keep someone else warm."

Emma's hands trembled as she clutched her phone, staring at the latest text from Luke. It was the same pattern as always: an accusation thinly veiled as concern, a reminder of how she had "failed" him, and the inevitable guilt trip that followed. Her chest tightened, and she felt that familiar wave of anxiety rising, like a dark cloud suffocating her from the inside.

She tossed the phone onto the couch, running her fingers through her hair as she tried to steady her breathing. It wasn't always like this. When she first met Luke three years ago, he had been charming, attentive, and everything she had ever wanted. But slowly, the charm gave way to criticism, the attentiveness turned into control, and the love she thought they shared morphed into something toxic and suffocating.

Emma looked over to the playroom where her two-year-old daughter, Lily, was playing. The soft sound of Lily's giggles momentarily pulled her out of her fog of anxiety. The little girl was blissfully unaware of the tension that seemed to fill every corner of their home these days. But Emma knew that wouldn't last forever. If things continued down this path, would Lily begin to notice? Worse, would she start to absorb the toxic atmosphere? Would it harm her emotionally? And while Luke had never laid a hand on Emma, she couldn't shake the fear that one day his anger could escalate and spill over to Lily.

Emma knew she wasn't herself anymore. She had become someone who constantly walked on eggshells, afraid of setting Luke off. She avoided her friends because she didn't want to answer their probing questions about why she looked so drained, why she never seemed happy anymore. Even though her work had begun to suffer, her once-sharp focus was clouded by the endless cycle of arguments, apologies, and the fleeting moments of peace that never lasted.

Luke was always sorry afterward. Always. But Emma had grown tired of the cycle. His apologies no longer brought her comfort or hope. Deep down, she knew that staying in this relationship might keep peace in the short term, but it could cost her much more in the long run, her happiness, her mental health, and perhaps even Lily's safety.

She had tried talking to Luke, tried to make him understand how his behavior affected her and, more importantly, how it might affect their daughter. But each time, he turned it around on her, making her feel like the problem was hers to fix. And each time, she had believed him, hoping that if she just tried a little harder, loved him a little more, things would get better.

But they never did.

Now, something inside her had snapped. The realization that she couldn't go on like this any longer had been creeping up on her for months, but now it was undeniable. She needed to make a change not just for herself, but for Lily as well.

Step 1: Define the Decision

The first and most crucial step in the decision-making process was to clearly define what decision needed to be made and the problem it aimed to solve. For Emma, the decision was about whether to continue her relationship with Luke or to end it. But as she delved deeper, she realized the complexity involved. This wasn't just about her relationship with Luke; it was also about the future well-being of her daughter, Lily.

She asked herself these key questions:

- What is the specific decision I need to make?

- What problem or opportunity am I addressing with this decision?

- What are the desired outcomes?

- Are there any underlying issues that need to be addressed first?

Emma understood that the decision to end the relationship wasn't just about her feelings toward Luke, it was about her mental health, her sense of self-worth, and her future happiness. But now, the stakes were even higher. She had to consider how staying in the relationship could affect Lily, both emotionally and possibly physically. Could the constant tension and Luke's anger harm Lily, even if he wasn't physically abusive? Could his behavior escalate in the future?

By clearly defining the decision, Emma would see that staying in the relationship might offer temporary relief, but it could erode her well-being and potentially Lily's in the long run.

Step 2: Gather Information

Once Emma had defined the decision, she knew she needed to gather more information, not just about her feelings and Luke's behavior but also about the impact it could have on Lily. She spent the next few days reflecting on the relationship. She thought about the early days when everything seemed perfect and compared them to the present, where the good moments were few and far between. She remembered the arguments, the times she had felt small and worthless, and the constant anxiety that had become a part of her daily life.

Most importantly, Emma began to pay closer attention to how the tension in the house might be affecting Lily. Was her bright, playful daughter starting to withdraw when Luke was around? Did she sense the underlying strain, even though she was too young to understand?

Emma also reached out to her best friend, Sarah, someone she had been avoiding out of embarrassment and fear of judgment. Sarah had always been supportive, but Emma had distanced herself as her relationship with Luke grew more toxic.

"Emma, what's going on?" Sarah's voice was full of concern when they finally spoke. "You've been so distant lately. Are you okay?"

Emma hesitated before answering. "No, I'm not okay, Sarah. I've been struggling a lot, and I think... I think I need to end things with

Luke. I'm worried about how this is all affecting Lily."

There was a long pause before Sarah responded. "I'm so sorry you've been going through this alone. But I'm glad you're telling me now. If you feel like it's time to end it, then it probably is. You deserve to be happy, Emma. And so does Lily. You deserve someone who loves you for who you are, not who they want you to be."

Hearing Sarah's words brought tears to Emma's eyes. She realized how much she had missed having someone to confide in, someone who saw her for who she really was, and who also recognized her responsibility as a mother.

Step 3: Weigh the Options

With the information she had gathered, Emma began to weigh her options. She made a list of the potential benefits and drawbacks of staying with Luke versus ending the relationship. The benefits of staying were clear: she wouldn't have to face the pain of a breakup, and she wouldn't have to uproot her, and Lily's lives. But the drawbacks were far more significant: continued emotional abuse, the further loss of her self-worth, the ongoing anxiety, and, most terrifying of all, the risk that Lily could be harmed emotionally, mentally, or even physically.

She also considered how ending the relationship could affect Lily. Would a breakup disrupt her sense of stability? Would it be confusing and painful for her? But then Emma reminded herself that staying in a toxic environment could be far worse for a child than the temporary discomfort of a breakup.

After some consideration, Emma realized that while staying with Luke might offer immediate comfort, the long-term consequences would be disastrous for her mental health and potentially for Lily's development. Ending the relationship would bring short-term pain, but it would also open the door to healing and regaining her sense of self. Most importantly, it would give Lily a chance to grow up in a healthier, more stable environment.

Step 4: Align with Values and Goals

Emma knew that any decision she made had to align with her core values and long-term goals. She valued her mental health, her independence, and her relationships with friends and family. But now, as a mother, her highest value was Lily's well-being and happiness. She wanted her daughter to grow up in an environment where she felt safe, loved, and free from the emotional toxicity that had taken over their home.

She reflected on how staying with Luke aligned with these values and goals. The answer was clear: it didn't. The relationship had isolated her from her friends, eroded her mental health, and made her feel small and unworthy. Even worse, it put Lily at risk of emotional harm.

On the other hand, ending the relationship would allow her to reconnect with her values and start building a life that aligned with her long-term goals, both for herself and for her daughter.

Step 5: Make the Decision

After gathering information, weighing the options, and ensuring alignment with her values and goals, Emma knew it was time to make a decision. She couldn't delay any longer. The offer of temporary comfort was tempting, but she knew that her long-term happiness, and Lily's well-being, was more important.

The next day, Emma decided to have the conversation with Luke. She didn't want to drag it out any longer, she needed to reclaim her life and protect her daughter. She rehearsed what she would say, knowing it wouldn't be easy but determined to be firm and clear.

That evening, Luke came over as usual, his expression guarded. He had sensed her growing distance, but he hadn't pushed her, yet. They sat on the couch, an awkward silence hanging between them until Emma finally spoke.

"Luke, we need to talk," she began, her voice steady despite the turmoil inside her. "I've been doing a lot of thinking, and I've realized that this relationship isn't healthy for me anymore. It's not healthy for Lily either."

Luke's eyes narrowed. "What are you talking about? We've had our problems, sure, but we've always worked through them."

Emma shook her head. "No, Luke, we haven't. We've been going in circles, and it's been hurting both of us. And I'm starting to worry about Lily. I can't keep doing this. I need to prioritize my well-being and Lily's."

Luke's expression hardened. "So, you're just going to walk away? After everything we've been through?"

"I'm not walking away from what we've been through," Emma said softly. "I'm walking away from what's been hurting me, and what could end up hurting Lily. I care about you, but I need to care about myself and my daughter more."

He stared at her, his anger slowly giving way to resignation. "You really mean it this time, don't you?"

"Yes, I do," Emma said, her voice trembling slightly but still firm. "I've made my decision."

Luke didn't argue further. He nodded, stood up, and walked out the door without another word. As the door clicked shut behind him, Emma felt a wave of relief wash over her, mingled with sadness and fear. But she knew it was the right choice, the only choice.

Step 6: Evaluate and Adjust

In the days that followed, Emma began to focus on healing. She reached out to friends she had lost touch with, explaining what had happened and slowly started rebuilding the connections she had neglected. She threw herself into her work, rediscovering the passion she had once felt for her career. Most importantly, she focused on Lily, spending time with her, playing with her, and making sure she felt loved and secure.

It wasn't easy. There were moments when Emma missed Luke, moments when she doubted whether she had made the right decision. But each time those doubts crept in, she reminded herself of why she had ended things, of the anxiety, the loss of self, and the toxicity that had overshadowed the good. She also made sure she kept Lily in mind, the sweet, innocent child who deserved to grow up in a loving, stable home.

Gradually, the cloud of anxiety that had hung over Emma began to lift. She started to feel like herself again, stronger, more confident in her ability to make decisions that were right for her and for her daughter. She wasn't just surviving anymore; she was beginning to thrive.

And for the first time in a long time, she felt hopeful about the future, both hers and Lily's.

Emma's story is a powerful reminder that not every relationship can or should be saved. Sometimes, the best decision is to let go of what no longer serves you and focus on creating a healthier, happier life now and in the future for yourself and your children.

Your Turn: Reflect, Consider and Decide

*"We do not learn from experiences...
we learn from reflecting on our experiences."*

Now that you've explored the decisions of Alyssa, David, and Emma, it's time to turn the reflection inward. Reflection plays a vital role in improving decision-making and aligning your choices with both present and future goals. Have you ever found yourself at a crossroads like Alyssa, considering an opportunity that offers short-term gains but carries long-term risks? Or maybe you resonate more with David, wondering if completing an old goal is still relevant. Perhaps Emma's story of reclaiming self-worth and prioritizing her mental health in a difficult relationship strikes a deeper chord.

Consider Your Past Decisions

Think about the significant decisions you've made in your life, whether in your career, relationships, or personal well-being. What was the basis of those choices? Did you focus more on immediate rewards, or were you thinking long-term? How have those decisions impacted you?

Did you benefit right away but face challenges later?

Or did you make sacrifices in the present for future gains?

Alyssa's story offers a real dilemma: taking a high-paying, prestigious job versus staying in a supportive, balanced environment. If you were in her shoes, would you prioritize higher salary and career growth, knowing the work environment could be toxic? Or would you lean toward keeping a stable, lower-stress job? How does the Win-When approach help you weigh both the short-term and long-term impact of such a choice?

Now, shift your focus to the decisions you are currently facing. Whether it's a career change, a financial investment, or a personal relationship, consider these choices through the lens of the Win-When approach:

- What are the immediate benefits of the decision?
- How will this choice shape your future and align with your long-term goals?
- Does this decision benefit your mental and emotional well-being now, as well as setting you up for future success?

Think about David, who had to decide whether finishing his degree would bring closure and personal satisfaction or add unnecessary stress to his well-established career and family life. Are there past goals or unfinished tasks in your life that you're still considering? Do they still align with your current values and future ambitions?

Or perhaps you relate more to Emma, whose decision to end a toxic relationship was difficult but necessary for her mental health and the well-being of her daughter. Have you ever faced a decision where staying put felt easier but ultimately harmful in the long run? How would the Win-When mindset help you navigate that situation and prioritize both your present and future self?

Reflecting on the Win-When Approach

Which aspects of the Win-When approach resonate most with you? Is it the focus on achieving balance between immediate benefits and long-term growth, or the importance of making decisions that align with your core values? Think about how applying this approach can help you improve not only the outcomes of your decisions but also your overall sense of control and fulfillment.

Stop and take some mental notes here.

Consider a recent decision you made. Did it align with the Win-When philosophy, and how it could have benefited you both now and later down the road?

What current decisions are you contemplating? How can you apply the Win-When approach to ensure you're making a choice that benefits both your present and your future?

By reflecting on your past choices and considering your present decisions through the Win-When lens, you'll find clarity. It's about balancing immediate needs with future aspirations and creating a life that benefits your current self and sets up your future self for success. This approach empowers you to make decisions that don't force you to sacrifice one for the other. Whether it's a career move, a personal relationship, or a significant life change, the Win-When approach guides you toward a future where both you and your loved ones will thrive.

As we close this chapter of reflection, it's essential to recognize that the power of decision-making lies not only in the outcomes we seek but also in the lessons learned along the way. Whether it's navigating Alyssa's career dilemma, David's choice to pursue or abandon an old goal, or Emma's courageous stand for her mental health and her

101

daughter's well-being, each story reveals the importance of balancing present and future needs.

Reflecting on your past decisions, whether good or bad, allows you to assess how well they served you both in the moment and down the line. Are there decisions you made for short-term rewards that left you with lasting challenges? Or choices that required present sacrifices but ultimately set you up for long-term success?

Now, consider the opportunities that may be awaiting you. Are you ready to take on new challenges, make bold choices, and apply the Win-When approach to seize them? Every opportunity carries the potential for both risk and reward. It's not just about jumping at the first chance; you must evaluate how it will serve you now and how it aligns with your future goals.

In the next chapter, we'll explore opportunities, those moments when a new path opens in your life. Have you ever had an opportunity you weren't sure how to handle? How did you approach it, and how would you handle the next challenge that comes your way? Let's dive into how you can apply the Win-When mindset to make the most of your opportunities while ensuring they contribute to both immediate success and future growth.

The Opportunity

*"There are really no failures,
just delayed successes."*

John Collins sat in his home office, the soft glow of the computer screen illuminating the room as the clock on the wall ticked past midnight. He was no stranger to late nights, but this one felt different. On his screen was a pitch deck, a well-crafted presentation detailing a promising new investment opportunity in a startup called Lumma Tech. His old friend and business partner, Mark, had brought it to his attention earlier that day, and ever since, John's mind had been racing.

Mark had always been the risk-taker, the one who thrived on the thrill of new ventures. Over the years, they have invested in several projects together, some had brought in substantial returns, while others had ended in disappointment. But this opportunity felt different. Lumma Tech was developing revolutionary energy-efficient technology, something that had the potential to disrupt an entire industry.

103

John, a seasoned investor with decades of experience, knew the potential rewards could be enormous. If Lumma Tech succeeded, the financial returns could be life changing. But he also understood the risks. The company was still in its infancy, with a promising prototype but little market presence. The financial commitment required was significant, and the possibility of losing everything was a real concern.

As he leaned back in his chair, John thought about his family. He had two children in college, with tuition bills that seemed to grow every semester. His wife, Laura, had been talking about their retirement plans, and they had both been looking forward to enjoying a slower pace of life in the coming years. Was this investment a smart move, or was it a gamble that could jeopardize their financial future?

He knew what he had to do; approach the decision with the same methodical, structured process he had used throughout his career.

Step 1: Define the Decision

The first step was for John to clearly define the decision he needed to make. It wasn't just about whether to invest in Lumma Tech or not, it was about understanding the broader implications of that choice. What problem or opportunity was he addressing with this decision? What were the desired outcomes?

He asked himself these vital questions:

- What is the specific decision I need to make?
- What problem or opportunity am I addressing with this decision?
- What are the desired outcomes?
- Are there any underlying issues that need to be addressed first?

John realized that the underlying issue was his desire to grow his investment portfolio while also securing his family's financial future. The opportunity presented by Lumma Tech was tempting, but it was important to ensure that the decision aligned with both his immediate needs and long-term goals.

The decision was not just about financial gain. It was about balancing the potential rewards with the risk of financial loss. It was about ensuring that any action he took today would support his future well-being.

Step 2: Gather Information

Once John had identified the decision, the next step was to gather as much information as possible. He needed to understand every aspect of Lumma Tech, the market potential, the strength of the team, the technology itself, and the financials.

The next morning, John met with Mark at their favorite restaurant for breakfast. Mark was already buzzing with excitement, going on about the potential markets Lumma Tech could tap into and the industry connections he had already made.

"John, this could be huge," Mark said, his enthusiasm evident. "I've spoken to some people in the industry, and they're all saying the same thing, that this technology is a game-changer. This is our opportunity to be getting in on the ground floor here."

John nodded, but he was not ready to be swept away by Mark's excitement. "I get it, Mark, and I'm intrigued. But we've been down this road before. I need to know more before I commit. What's their burn rate? How long until they run out of cash if things don't go as planned? And what about the team? Are they experienced enough to handle the challenges ahead?"

Mark's optimism didn't waver. "I've met the founder, Jake. He's sharp, driven, and has a solid track record in the industry. The team is small but capable. They're all in this for the long haul. And as for the finances, they've got enough runway for the next 18 months, assuming they stick to the current budget. If we come in, we can help them extend that runway and get them to the next round of funding."

John appreciated Mark's confidence, but his instinct told him to dig deeper. He spent the next week immersing himself in all things Lumma Tech. He analyzed the financials, scrutinized the business plan, and researched the market. He also met with Jake, the founder, who impressed him with his vision and technical expertise. Jake's passion for the technology was evident, and his commitment to seeing it succeed was clear.

John also spoke with a few of the engineers, who were equally enthusiastic about the project. They explained the challenges they faced and how they were overcoming them, giving John a better sense of the team's capabilities.

But even with all the information he had gathered, John still felt a knot of uncertainty in his stomach. The startup world is notoriously unpredictable, and while Lumma Tech had potential, there were no guarantees. Investing at such an early stage with this company meant that success could take years, or it might never come at all.

Step 3: **Weigh the Options**

With all the information in hand, John began to weigh his options. The benefits of investing in Lumma Tech were clear: the potential for significant financial returns, the opportunity to be part of an innovative company, and the excitement of supporting a technology that could change the world. However, the risks were equally clear; the possibility of losing his investment, the uncertainty of the startup's future, and the impact it could have on his family's financial security was very real.

John considered these key questions:

- What are the specific investment options available to me for Lumma Tech?

- Should I invest a significant portion of my savings in Lumma Tech, invest a smaller, more conservative amount, or not invest at all to preserve my family's financial security?

- How does each option fit with my personal values and financial goals?
- What are the short-term and long-term consequences of each investment decision?

- In the short term, will investing heavily in Lumma Tech strain our finances and create additional stress, or will it provide a thrilling opportunity for financial growth?

- In the long term, will a larger investment jeopardize our ability to comfortably pay for our children's college education and fund our retirement, or could it secure life-changing returns? Would a more conservative investment allow for both growth and security over time?

He realized that while the potential rewards of investing in Lumma Tech were high, the financial risk was also significant. If the company succeeded, the investment could pay off in a big way. But if it failed, the loss could have serious consequences for his family's financial future.

He considered the option of investing a smaller amount, one that would allow him to be part of the venture without putting his family's security at risk. This approach would reduce the potential rewards, but it would also minimize the impact if the company didn't succeed.

Step 4: Align with Values and Goals

As John continued to weigh his options, he knew that any decision he made had to align with his core values and long-term goals. He valued financial security, stability, and the ability to provide for his family. He also valued taking calculated risks and seizing opportunities for growth.

He reflected on how investing in Lumma Tech aligned with what he needed. The opportunity to be part of groundbreaking technology was exciting, and the potential financial rewards would support his long-term goals. But he also knew that the risk of losing his investment could jeopardize the financial stability he had worked so hard to achieve.

He asked himself these critical questions:

- Investing in Lumma Tech could offer significant rewards, but does it uphold my commitment to ensuring financial stability for my family, especially with tuition bills and retirement approaching?

- How does this choice support my long-term goal of securing my family's future while pursuing investment opportunities?

- Will this decision allow me to continue building the balanced life I want for my family, without risking the stability we've worked hard to create?

- Does investing in Lumma Tech help me move toward the lifestyle my wife and I envision for our retirement, or does it introduce unnecessary financial risks that could compromise our plans?

- Are there any potential conflicts between this decision and my goals of financial security and responsible risk-taking?

John realized that while he believed in Lumma Tech's potential, he couldn't ignore the risks. To align the decision with his values, he needed to find a way to invest in the company without compromising his family's financial security. This meant taking a more conservative approach, one that allowed him to participate in the venture without putting everything on the line.

Step 5: Make the Decision

After gathering information, weighing the options, and ensuring alignment with his values and goals, it was time to make a decision. John considered all of the relevant factors and was ready to commit to a course of action.

That evening, he sat down with his wife, Laura, to discuss the situation. They had always made major decisions together, and he valued her perspective very much.

"Laura, I've been going back and forth on this Lumma Tech investment," John began, running a hand through his graying hair. "There's a lot of potential, but it's a big risk. I don't want to jeopardize our financial security, especially with the kids' tuition and our retirement plans."

Laura listened carefully; her brow furrowed in thought. "John, you've always been smart about these things. You've taken risks before, but you've always made sure they were calculated. Do you believe in this company? Do you think it's worth the risk?"

John paused, considering her words. "I do believe in it, but I also know there's a chance it could fail. I've vetted the company thoroughly, and everything checks out. The technology is solid, and the team is capable. But it's still a startup, and we know how unpredictable that can be."

Laura reached out and took his hand. "Then maybe it's about balancing the risk. How much would you need to invest to feel like you're giving it a real chance? And how much can we afford to lose if things don't go as planned?"

John nodded slowly. "That's what I've been thinking about. If we go in, it needs to be an amount that won't cripple us if it's lost. Something that gives us a stake in the company but still leaves us with enough security."

Laura smiled, her eyes full of trust. "Then do that. If you believe in this venture, take the leap, but do it in a way that keeps us safe, too. We've always been in this together, and I know you'll make the right choice."

John felt a sense of clarity as he listened to Laura's words. He had done his due diligence, vetted the startup, and carefully weighed the potential rewards against the risks. The decision was no longer about whether to invest, but how much to invest.

The next day, John called Mark. "After careful consideration, I'm willing to invest because I believe in the long-term potential of this venture. But I'm going in with a conservative amount. I want to be part of this, but I need to protect our financial future as well."

Mark was understanding and supportive. "I get it, John. I'm glad you're on board, even if it's with a smaller stake. We'll make it work."

Step 6: Evaluate and Adjust

With the decision made, John finalized the investment, becoming a part of the Lumma Tech family. As the months passed, he watched the company grow, facing the ups and downs that came with the startup territory. There were moments of doubt, times when the challenges seemed insurmountable, but John remained committed to the venture, knowing that he had made the right decision.

Lumma Tech eventually secured additional funding, allowing them to expand their operations and bring their technology closer to market. The investment began to show signs of paying off, though the road was still long and uncertain. But through it all, John remained at peace with his choice.

He took a calculated risk, one that balanced his belief in the company with the need to safeguard his family's financial future. He didn't let fear dictate his actions, nor did he leap blindly into a venture that could have jeopardized everything he had worked for. Instead, he navigated the decision with the wisdom that came from years of experience, ensuring that his present actions aligned with his long-term goals.

Leveraging the Win-When Concepts

John's decision to invest in Lumma Tech exemplifies the Win-When concepts in action. Faced with an opportunity that carried both high potential rewards and significant risks, John didn't rush into a decision based solely on the promise of future gains. Instead, he thoroughly vetted the startup, weighing the credibility of the team, the soundness of the technology, and the financial realities.

The Win-When approach emphasizes the importance of balancing immediate actions with long-term well-being and success. John embodied this by choosing to invest in a way that allowed him to participate in the venture's potential upside without putting his family's financial security at undue risk. He recognized that while the opportunity was promising, the unpredictability of the startup world necessitated a cautious approach.

John demonstrated personal accountability, another core principle of the Win-When mindset. He took ownership of the decision-making process, gathering all the necessary information and consulting with trusted individuals, including his wife. By doing so, he ensured that the decision to invest was not only well-informed but also aligned with his broader life goals.

In the end, John's story is proof that the power of thoughtful, deliberate decision-making yields solid outcomes. By leveraging the Win-When principles, he was able to pursue a promising opportunity without compromising his long-term security. His journey serves as a reminder that in both life and business, the best decisions are those that consider both the present and the future, ensuring that success is sustainable over time.

Take The Money And Stay

*"A good woman follows the rules,
A great woman follows herself."*

Maya Bennett sat at her desk, staring at the email that had just come through. Her heart raced as she scanned the words for the third time. It was the moment she had been waiting for; a promotion to Vice President of Operations at her tech firm, Halcyon Enterprises. This was her dream job, the career leap she had worked so hard for over the past decade. Yet, despite the excitement welling inside her, there was a catch, the role required her to relocate to the company's new headquarters in Seattle.

Maya leaned back in her chair, her mind spinning. She lives in Chicago, close to her aging parents. Her father's health had been declining, and she had stepped into the role of partial caretaker, helping her mother manage the increasing strain of looking after him. Moving to Seattle would mean leaving her family behind, and the thought of being so far away from them tugged at her heart.

117

The promotion was a significant career advancement, with a hefty salary increase, new challenges, and the chance to lead a larger team. But the personal cost weighed heavily on her. Could she balance her career ambitions with her family responsibilities? And if she moved, how would she manage the guilt of leaving her parents behind?

Step 1: Define the Decision

Maya knew she couldn't rush this decision. The first thing she needed to do was clearly define what she was deciding. It wasn't just about accepting a promotion or declining it. It was about whether she was willing to move across the country and how that would impact her family life. The problem was bigger than a simple yes or no.

As she sat down with her journal, Maya wrote down her thoughts. What was the decision she needed to make? She realized the core issue wasn't just about the job; it was about whether she could handle the personal impact of moving far away from her family, particularly her parents, who relied on her. This decision wasn't just about her career, it was about balancing her future professional goals with her present family obligations.

Key questions filled her mind:

- What problem or opportunity was she addressing?

- What were the real issues behind her hesitation?

- What were her desired outcomes, both personally and professionally?

The clarity of the decision allowed Maya to see that the promotion was a huge career opportunity, but it came with significant personal consequences. She needed to dig deeper into what mattered most to her.

Step 2: Gather Information

Once Maya had defined the decision, the next step was to gather the relevant information. She needed a clear picture of what moving to Seattle would mean for her career, her parents, and her personal life. She began by researching the specifics of the promotion: the job role, responsibilities, and the company's long-term plans for the new headquarters.

She then reached out to Erica, her mentor and the VP of Human Resources at Halcyon Enterprises. Erica had always been a source of wisdom and guidance, and Maya trusted her judgment. Over coffee, Maya explained her situation, her excitement about the promotion, and her concerns about leaving her parents behind.

119

"I understand how tough this is," Erica said thoughtfully. "The promotion is a fantastic opportunity, and it would be a great step in your career. But I also know how important family is to you, and it's not easy to be far away when they need you. Have you considered compromise? Maybe you could negotiate a hybrid work situation where you split your time between Chicago and Seattle?"

Maya hadn't considered that possibility. Erica's suggestion opened a new avenue for her decision. She also talked to her parents to understand their perspective. Her mother, though supportive of her career, expressed concerns about managing her father's care without Maya's regular help.

With this new information, Maya felt better equipped to make her decision. She had a clearer understanding of what the role entailed and how her family would cope if she moved.

Step 3: Weigh the Options

Armed with the facts, Maya now had to weigh her options carefully. The promotion offered her the chance to grow in her career, increase her financial security, and expand her professional network. On the other hand, moving would put her far from her parents at a time when they needed her most.

She made a list of pros and cons, detailing the short-term and long-term consequences of each option:

Option 1: Accept Promotion and Relocate

Pros: Career growth, financial gain, increased professional influence, a new city with exciting opportunities.

Cons: Leaving her parents, potential feelings of guilt and worry, adapting to a new city, and the emotional strain of being far from her family.

Option 2: Decline the Promotion

Pros: Stay close to her parents, maintain her current support system, and avoid the stress of relocation.

Cons: Missed career opportunity, potential for career stagnation, and loss of the chance to lead a larger team.

Maya also considered Erica's suggestion of negotiating a hybrid role, which would allow her to take the promotion but not completely leave her family behind. This third option seemed like the best of both worlds, but it required further negotiation.

Step 4: Align with Values and Goals

Maya knew she needed to align her decision with her core values and long-term goals. She had always valued family deeply, and caring for her parents was a priority. But her career was also important to her, and she had worked tirelessly to get to this point.

She asked herself:

- What were her values in this situation? Family, career growth, and personal fulfillment.

- How would this decision support her long-term goals of leadership and financial independence?

- Would the choice she made now bring her closer to the life she wanted?

The promotion aligned perfectly with her professional goals, but the thought of leaving her family made her feel uneasy. Her core values of family and career success seemed to be in conflict, but Maya knew she needed to find a way to honor both.

After much reflection, she realized that her ideal decision would allow her to advance in her career while still being there for her parents. The hybrid work model emerged as the solution that best aligned with her values and goals.

Step 5: Make the Decision

After weeks of reflection, Maya decided to pursue the hybrid option. She called her boss, Dan, and scheduled a meeting to discuss her decision. As she sat across from Dan, she explained her situation clearly and confidently.

"I'm really excited about the opportunity to step into the VP role and contribute to Halcyon's growth in Seattle," Maya began. "However, my parents are up in age, and I'm involved in helping care for my father. That's why I'd like to discuss the possibility of a hybrid work arrangement, splitting my time between Seattle and Chicago so I can still support my family while taking on this new challenge."

Dan was thoughtful as he listened. "I understand where you're coming from, Maya. Family is important, and we value you here at Halcyon. Let me talk to the leadership team and see what we can work out. We want to make sure this promotion is a positive step for you in all aspects."

Maya felt a sense of relief wash over her. She had made her decision, and now it was up to the company to see if they could meet her halfway.

Step 6: Evaluate and Adjust

A week later, Dan called Maya with good news. The company had agreed to her hybrid work arrangement. She would spend two weeks each month in Seattle and two weeks working remotely from Chicago. This way, she could manage her new responsibilities while still being close to her parents.

Maya felt a wave of gratitude. The hybrid model wasn't a perfect solution, there would still be challenges in balancing her time, but it allowed her to pursue her career goals without sacrificing her family obligations.

Over the next few months, Maya adjusted to her new role. There were times when the trip felt exhausting, and she missed the consistency of being in one place. But she knew that the decision she had made was the right one for her. She regularly checked in with her parents, and while the distance was tough, they had found a new routine that worked.

Maya also kept a close eye on how the hybrid arrangement impacted her performance at work. She stayed in constant communication with her team, ensuring that her time in

Seattle was productive and her time in Chicago was focused. If she felt the balance slipping, she made small adjustments, setting clearer boundaries, delegating more tasks, or arranging longer stays in Seattle during critical project phases.

Leveraging the Win-When Concepts

Maya's journey is a powerful example of how to leverage the Win-When concepts in decision-making. Throughout the process, she applied the structured decision-making framework to ensure that her choice aligned with both her present needs and long-term goals.

Maya took the time to clearly define what was at stake, not just a job promotion, but the balance between her career and family obligations. This clarity helped her see the real issue she was grappling with, allowing her to approach the decision from a holistic perspective.

Maya didn't rush into the decision. She gathered all the information she could, talking to her mentor, consulting with her parents, and researching the logistics of the promotion and relocation. This thorough approach ensured that she was making a well-informed decision.

Instead of focusing solely on the career benefits, Maya carefully weighed the pros and cons of each option, considering both the short-term and long-term consequences. By doing so, she was able to see the potential impact on her personal life and find a middle ground that would work for her.

Maya's decision was guided by her core values, family, career growth, and personal fulfillment. She didn't compromise on her values, instead finding a solution that allowed her to honor both her family obligations and her career aspirations.

Once Maya had gathered the information and weighed her options, she confidently made her decision. She communicated her needs clearly to her employer and negotiated a hybrid work model that worked for both her and the company.

After the decision was implemented, Maya continued to evaluate how it was working. She made adjustments when necessary, ensuring that both her family and her career continued to thrive.

In the end, Maya's story demonstrates the power of making deliberate, informed decisions that are aligned with both immediate and long-term goals.

The Spark of an Idea

*"I would love to stay but that would
keep me from leaving."*

Amara Davis sat at her kitchen table, the soft hum of the city outside the window, a distant backdrop to the whirlwind of thoughts racing through her mind. Before her, lay a notebook, its pages covered in her scribbles, sketches, and ideas that had consumed her for years now. At 36, Amara had spent the last decade working as the marketing director for a well-established tech firm, a position that provided her with a steady paycheck, a solid benefits package, and a clear path to further advancement. Yet, for all the security it offered, her job no longer felt fulfilling.

Over time, what had once been a source of excitement and growth now felt monotonous. The corporate environment that had once inspired her now stifled her creativity, and her responsibilities, though challenging, no longer sparked joy. There was something bigger calling to her, something she knew she could build if only she had the courage to pursue it.

In the pages of her notebook, the idea had taken shape: a platform that would provide affordable, customizable marketing solutions for startups and small businesses, companies that couldn't afford the hefty fees charged by big marketing agencies. Amara believed that with the right approach, she could help these companies succeed while filling a gap in the market.

The idea had blossomed into something more than just a passing thought, it was a vision, one she believed had the potential to change her life. But turning that vision into reality meant leaving behind the safety net of her current job, and that was where her excitement met its equal in fear.

Amara was torn. The thought of leaving her stable, well-paying job filled her with dread. What if the business failed? What if she ended up draining her savings on something that never took off? But at the same time, the idea of staying where she was, knowing she had the potential to do more, filled her with an equally unsettling sense of regret.

As she sat in her kitchen, the choice before her seemed monumental. She had to decide, stay in her comfort zone or take the leap into the unknown.

Step 1: Define the Decision

Before diving into any decision, Amara knew she had to define what she was deciding. Was it as simple as choosing between staying at her job or starting her business? Or was there more at stake? As she reflected on this, Amara realized the decision was about more than just her career. It was about what kind of life she wanted to build for herself, the balance she wanted between security and passion, and the role she wanted her work to play in her overall happiness.

She wrote down the key questions that would guide her decision:

- What problem was she addressing with this decision?

- What were the desired outcomes, both personally and professionally?

- Were there underlying issues that needed to be addressed, like her dissatisfaction with her current role?

By clearly defining the decision, Amara could see it wasn't just about quitting her job or starting a business. It was about pursuing a career that aligned with her passion for helping others, one that would allow her to make a meaningful impact while also achieving personal fulfillment. This clarity helped her move forward with purpose.

Step 2: Gather Information

With a clear understanding of her decision, Amara moved to the next step: gathering information. She needed to know what starting her own business would entail, the risks, the costs, the opportunities, and whether she was truly ready for it. She began researching the market for customizable marketing platforms, analyzing potential competitors, and speaking with small business owners to gauge their interest.

But Amara knew that research alone wouldn't answer all her questions. She needed insight from someone who had been where she was now. That's when she reached out to Lisa, her longtime mentor and a successful entrepreneur who had built her own marketing firm from the ground up. They met at a cozy restaurant downtown, where Amara poured out her excitement and fears over the business idea.

"Lisa, I've been thinking about this for months now," Amara said, stirring her coffee nervously. "I really believe in the potential of this platform, but I'm terrified of leaving my job. What if I fail? What if I drain my savings and the business doesn't take off?"

Lisa listened carefully with a thoughtful look on her face. "Every entrepreneur has those fears, Amara. There's always a risk when you leave something stable for the unknown. But the question you need to ask yourself is this: Are you willing to take that risk to pursue something you're passionate about? Do you believe in your idea enough to see it through, even when things get tough?"

Amara nodded slowly. "I do believe in it. But the financial uncertainty is hard to ignore."

"That's understandable," Lisa said. "But have you looked into securing outside funding? Investors, loans, or even grants could help you get started without putting all the pressure on your savings. You don't have to shoulder all the financial risk yourself."

Amara hadn't considered that option. The thought of taking on debt or giving up equity in her business had seemed daunting, but Lisa's suggestion made sense. There were ways to mitigate the financial risks if she took the time to explore them.

Step 3: Weigh the Options

Armed with new information, Amara spent the next few weeks weighing her options. She dove into researching funding opportunities, meeting with potential investors, and even attending a few networking events for entrepreneurs. One of the most promising leads came from a local startup accelerator that offered seed funding and mentorship in exchange for a small equity stake.

The program was designed to help entrepreneurs like Amara get their ideas off the ground, providing not only financial backing but also the resources and guidance she would need to launch successfully. The seed funding would cover her initial expenses, allowing her to pursue the business without draining her savings. In exchange, she would give up a small percentage of ownership—a trade-off that felt worth it for the support and security the accelerator would provide.

Now, Amara has two clear options:

- **Option 1:** Stay at her current job, continuing to earn a stable salary but at the cost of her passion and fulfillment.

- **Option 2:** Take the leap, leave her job, and pursue her business idea with the backing of the accelerator program, knowing there were risks but also the potential for high reward.

She weighed the short-term and long-term consequences of each choice. Staying in her job would provide her with financial security, but it would also leave her feeling unfulfilled. Starting her business was riskier, but it aligned more closely with her long-term goals of making a meaningful impact in the small business world.

Step 4: Align with Values and Goals

One evening, Amara sat down with her notebook and reflected on her core values. What truly mattered to her? The answer was clear: she valued creativity, independence, and making a difference in the lives of others. Helping small businesses thrive was something that ignited her passion, and her current job wasn't providing that sense of purpose anymore.

She also thought about her long-term goals. She wanted to build something of her own, something that combined her love for technology and marketing with her desire to help entrepreneurs succeed. Staying at her current job, while comfortable, wouldn't get her there.

The business idea, however, fits perfectly with both her values and her goals. It would allow her to channel her creativity, take control of her career, and make a tangible difference in the world. The more she thought about it, the more she realized that this was the path she needed to take.

Step 5: Make the Decision

After weeks of reflection, market research, and discussions, Amara felt ready to make her decision. She would take the leap and pursue her dream of starting her own business. But first, she had to tell her boss, Greg, about her decision to leave the company.

The thought of having this conversation filled her with dread. Greg had been a supportive and fair manager, and she didn't want to disappoint him. But she also knew that this was the right choice for her future.

She scheduled a meeting with Greg and rehearsed what she would say. When the day finally arrived, she walked into his office with a sense of resolve.

"Greg, thank you for making time to meet with me," Amara began, her voice steady despite her nerves. "There's something important I need to talk to you about."

Greg looked up, curious. "Of course, Amara. What's on your mind?"

Taking a deep breath, she continued. "I've been working on a business idea that I'm really passionate about. It combines my experience in marketing with my desire to help small businesses succeed. After a lot of thought, I've decided that it's time for me to pursue this dream full-time."

Greg raised his eyebrows in surprise but quickly smiled. "Wow, Amara, that's a big decision. I didn't know you were thinking about starting your own business."

"I've kept it under wraps until I was certain," Amara explained. "But I'm confident in the plan, and I've secured financial backing. I'm ready to take the leap and launch this business because I believe in its potential."

Greg nodded, taking it all in. "I'm proud of you, Amara. It takes a lot of courage to leave a stable job and venture out on your own. Of course, we'll be sad to lose you, but I understand why you need to do this. Do you have a timeline in mind?"

Amara felt a wave of relief at Greg's supportive response. "I'd like to transition over the next few weeks to ensure everything is in good hands before I leave."

"That sounds fair," Greg agreed. "We'll work together to make sure the transition is smooth. And if you ever need anything, don't hesitate to reach out."

Step 6: Evaluate and Adjust

The final step in the decision-making process was to evaluate the outcome of her decision and adjust as needed. After leaving her job and joining the startup accelerator, Amara threw herself into building her business. The months that followed were filled with long hours, challenges, and moments of doubt. But as she continued to grow her platform and secure clients, her confidence grew.

The accelerator provided her with invaluable resources, from legal advice to marketing strategies. And while there were still hurdles to overcome, Amara knew she had made the right decision. She regularly checked in with her mentors and adjusted her strategies based on the feedback she received. If something wasn't working, she pivoted. If an opportunity arose, she seized it.

Through it all, Amara remained focused on the long-term vision she had for her business. There were times when the uncertainty felt overwhelming, but she stayed committed to the decision she had made, knowing that she had approached it with care, intention, and a clear process.

Leveraging the Win-When Concepts

Amara's journey to start her own business is a prime example of how the "Win-When" decision-making process can guide individuals through major life changes. Rather than rushing into the decision or making a choice based on fear, Amara carefully applied each step of the process to ensure her decision was aligned with both her immediate and long-term goals.

Amara took the time to understand the true nature of the decision she was making. It wasn't just about leaving a job; it was about pursuing a life and career that aligned with her values and passions.

She didn't make the decision lightly. She gathered as much information as possible, from market research to mentorship, ensuring she had a complete picture of what she was getting into.

Amara carefully considered the short-term and long-term consequences of both staying in her job and pursuing her business. She weighed the risks and benefits and sought out funding options to mitigate financial risk.

The decision to start her own business aligned with her core values of creativity, independence, and helping others. It also supported her long-term goals of building something meaningful and impactful.

Once she had all the information and weighed her options, Amara confidently made the decision to leave her job and pursue her business. She communicated her decision clearly and effectively, ensuring a smooth transition.

After making the decision, Amara continued to evaluate the outcome and adjust her approach as needed. This flexibility allowed her to navigate the challenges of entrepreneurship while staying focused on her long-term success.

By following the Win-When decision-making process, Amara was able to turn her dream into reality while balancing risk and reward. Her story is a testament to the power of structured decision-making, and it serves as a guide for anyone facing major life choices.

Self-Reflections

"When you truly reflect, you don't just see yourself; you understand the person you've been all along."

In the last three chapters, we followed the journeys of three individuals, John, Maya, and Amara, as they navigated significant, life-changing decisions. Each story illustrates how the Win-When approach guided them toward choices that aligned with their core values and long-term goals. This approach isn't about seeking quick wins or immediate gratification, but about building a foundation for sustained success that reflects who you are and what truly matters to you.

In John's story, we saw how a seasoned investor faced the temptation of a high-reward opportunity with the potential to disrupt his financial stability. John, a family man, was presented with an offer to invest in Lumma Tech, a promising startup in the energy sector.

As exciting as the opportunity was, John was equally aware of the risks involved. With two children in college and retirement on the horizon, the consequences of a failed

139

investment could be disastrous. John took a measured approach, relying on the Win-When process to guide him through the decision.

John defined the decision clearly, this wasn't just about whether or not to invest, but about how to protect his family's financial security while still allowing room for growth. He gathered as much information as possible, researching the company's potential, meeting the team, and assessing the risks.

After weighing his options, John chose to invest a conservative amount, ensuring his family's security even if the investment didn't pay off. As Lumma Tech grew, John regularly evaluated the investment's performance, ready to make adjustments when necessary.

John's story is a prime example of how the Win-When approach ensures that decisions are aligned with both short-term and long-term needs. Rather than focusing solely on potential financial gain, he balanced the risks with the need to safeguard his family's future. John's decision wasn't just about securing a win in the present, it was about making a choice that would continue to benefit him and his loved ones in the years to come.

Maya's story took us through a different kind of balancing act. As a successful professional, Maya was offered a dream promotion to Vice President of Operations, a role that came with a significant salary increase and career advancement.

However, accepting the promotion meant relocating across the country, far from her aging parents who relied on her for support. Torn between her career ambitions and family obligations, Maya faced a difficult choice.

Maya understood that this decision wasn't just about whether or not to take the promotion, but about finding a way to honor both her professional goals and her responsibility to her family. She gathered information from her mentors, family members, and her employer, exploring the possibility of a hybrid work arrangement.

Maya carefully weighed the pros and cons of each option, considering how her decision would impact both her career and her family. In the end, she chose to negotiate a flexible work model that allowed her to split her time between two cities, balancing her professional aspirations with her family responsibilities.

Maya's story reflects the core of the Win-When approach: aligning decisions with your values. She didn't rush into a choice that would have compromised her relationship with her family or her career. Instead, she found a way to ensure both aspects of her life could thrive, embodying the principle that success doesn't have to come at the cost of what's most important to you.

Amara's journey was rooted in her desire for fulfillment and independence. After spending years in a stable corporate role, Amara realized that her current job no longer sparked the passion and creativity it once had.

She had an idea for a business, an affordable, customizable marketing platform, but the fear of leaving her secure position held her back. Amara faced the daunting decision of whether to stay in the comfort of her job or take the leap into entrepreneurship.

For Amara, defining the decision meant understanding that this was about more than just changing jobs, it was about pursuing a career that aligned with her values of creativity, independence, and helping others.

She gathered information through market research, mentorship, and funding options to ensure she was prepared for the risks ahead. After carefully weighing the benefits and challenges of each option, Amara chose to leave her job and pursue her passion, securing seed funding from a startup accelerator to help mitigate the financial risk.

Amara's story is a testament to how the Win-When approach can help guide you through uncertainty. By aligning her decision with her values and long-term goals, she didn't let fear stand in the way of pursuing a career that was more fulfilling. Her journey shows that even in the face of risk, when your decisions are grounded in what truly matters to you, they are more likely to lead to lasting success.

As you reflect on these stories, consider the decisions you've made or are about to make in your own life.

- How often have your choices been aligned with your core values?

- Have you taken the time to clearly define the decisions in front of you, gathering all the necessary information before weighing your options?

- And most importantly, do your decisions reflect not only what you need right now, but also what you want for your future?

The Win-When approach isn't just about securing success in the present and future, it's about ensuring that your decisions resonate with who you are and where you're headed. Whether you're facing a career change, a financial decision, or a personal challenge, ask yourself: Are my decisions aligned with my values and long-term goals? The more deliberate and value-driven your choices are, the more likely they are to lead to meaningful, sustained success now and in the years to come.

As we move into the next few chapters, we'll explore some of the most pivotal and impactful decisions you'll ever face, decisions that can shape your financial and personal future in profound ways.

First, we'll look at the delicate task of managing a windfall. Whether it's from an inheritance, a sudden career opportunity, or a major financial gain, deciding how to handle this unexpected wealth can lead to either long-term security or fleeting satisfaction.

Next, we'll tackle a decision that tests your core values. How do you weigh opportunity against what you believe in? We'll dive into examples of value-driven decision-making and explore how to navigate these challenging situations without compromising your integrity.

Lastly, we'll examine how to decide when to hold onto a strong financial investment and when it's time to let go. This is one of the toughest decisions for any investor.

Each of these upcoming chapters will challenge you to think deeply about your decisions and how to maintain a balance between your values, present satisfaction, and future success.

The Unexpected Gift

*"Don't look a gift horse in the mouth,
but if you do, smile back."*

Jasmine Henderson was sitting at her desk, lost in the minutiae of another workday, when her phone buzzed with an incoming call. Glancing at the screen, she saw that it was her Aunt Joanne, a call she wasn't expecting. Joanne was the matriarch of the family, the one who had always been there with advice and support. But her tone was different this time, somber, with a gravity that Jasmine hadn't heard before.

"Jasmine, I have some news," Joanne began. "Your Uncle Mike passed away last night."

The words hit Jasmine like a punch to the gut. Uncle Mike had been one of the kindest, most generous people she had ever known. He wasn't just a relative; he had been a mentor, someone who had always encouraged her to dream big and stay grounded. Even though they hadn't seen each other often in recent years, his presence in her life had always been a comforting constant.

"I'm so sorry, Aunt Joanne," Jasmine said, her voice thick with emotion. "I can't believe it."

"I know, sweetheart," Joanne replied. "He went peacefully in his sleep. But there's something else you need to know. Mike left you something in his will. It's... significant."

Jasmine didn't know what to say. She had no idea what her aunt meant by "significant," but she didn't care about the money. She was mourning her uncle, not thinking about finances.

"Aunt Joanne, that's... I don't even know what to say."

"You don't have to say anything right now, Jasmine. But you should be prepared. Mike had quite a bit set aside, and he wanted you to have it. He always believed in you; you know."

Jasmine felt tears welling up in her eyes. "I'll take care of it, Aunt Joanne. Thank you for letting me know."

After the call ended, Jasmine sat in silence for a long time, trying to process the loss and the unexpected windfall that was about to come her way. She couldn't shake the feeling that this was a pivotal moment in her life, one that required careful thought and responsibility.

The Weight of Wealth

A few weeks later, after the funeral and the reading of the will, Jasmine found herself sitting in a lawyer's office, staring at a number that didn't seem real. Uncle Mike had left her $500,000, a staggering amount of money that could change her life in countless ways.

She felt a mix of emotions: gratitude, disbelief, and an overwhelming sense of responsibility. This was a gift from someone she loved, and she didn't want to squander it. But at the same time, she couldn't help but think about all the things she could do with the money, pay off her student loans, buy a new car, take a much-needed vacation, maybe even put a down payment on a house.

The possibilities were endless, and that was both exciting and terrifying.

As she walked out of the lawyer's office, the check securely in her purse, Jasmine knew she needed to make a plan. This wasn't money to be spent frivolously; it was a chance to secure her financial future, to honor her uncle's memory by making smart, deliberate choices.

But where to start? She had never dealt with this kind of money before, and the pressure to make the right decisions weighed heavily on her.

Seeking Guidance

Jasmine knew she couldn't navigate this new reality alone, so she reached out to someone she trusted—her financial advisor, Karen Mitchell. Karen had been working with Jasmine for a few years, helping her manage her modest savings and guiding her toward her financial goals. But this was a whole new ball game, and Jasmine needed Karen's expertise more than ever.

They met over dinner, and Jasmine wasted no time in laying out the situation.

"Karen, I just inherited $500,000 from my uncle," Jasmine said, her voice still tinged with disbelief. "I've never had this kind of money before, and I don't want to mess it up. I need your help figuring out what to do."

Karen nodded, her expression thoughtful. "First of all, I'm sorry for your loss, Jasmine. It sounds like your uncle thought very highly of you to leave you such a significant amount. You're right to want to handle this carefully."

"Thank you," Jasmine replied. "I just don't know where to start. Part of me wants to pay off all my debts and take a trip, but I also know this could be a chance to really secure my future."

"You're thinking about it the right way," Karen said. "The first thing we need to do is establish your priorities. What are your long-term goals? What do you want this money to do for you?"

Jasmine took a moment to think. "I want to be debt-free, that's for sure. But I also want to start saving for a down payment on a house. And I'd like to invest some of it, to make sure it keeps growing. But I also want to enjoy it a little, maybe take that trip I've been dreaming about."

Karen smiled. "That's a good balance. The key is to make sure you're setting yourself up for long-term success while allowing yourself to enjoy the present. We can create a plan that covers all those bases."

They spent the next hour discussing options. Karen suggested that Jasmine start by paying off her student loans and credit card debt, an immediate way to improve her financial health. They also talked about setting aside a portion of the money for a down payment on a house, investing in a diversified portfolio, and creating an emergency fund.

As for the trip, Karen encouraged Jasmine to set aside a small percentage of the windfall, perhaps 10%, to spend on something that brought her joy.

"This is about balance," Karen said. "You don't want to blow through the money, but you also don't want to feel like you're not allowed to enjoy any of it. Your uncle gave you this gift to help you, not to make you feel burdened by it."

Jasmine left the meeting feeling more confident. She had a plan, and it was one that honored both her present desires and her future needs.

The Plan in Action

With Karen's guidance, Jasmine began to put her plan into action. The first step was paying off her student loans and credit card debt, a move that immediately lifted a weight off her shoulders. For the first time in years, she was debt-free, and the sense of relief was overwhelming.

Next, she set up an emergency fund, enough to cover six months of living expenses. It was a safety net that gave her peace of mind, knowing she had a cushion to fall back on in case of unexpected expenses or life changes.

Jasmine also worked with Karen to invest a significant portion of the windfall. They focused on a diversified portfolio that included stocks, crypto, and mutual funds, ensuring that her money would continue to grow over time. It was an investment strategy that aligned with her long-term goals, providing a foundation for her future financial security.

But Jasmine didn't stop there. She also set aside a portion of the money for a down payment on a house. It was a dream she always had, owning a home of her own, a place where she could build a life and create lasting memories. With the windfall, that dream was now within reach.

Finally, Jasmine allowed herself to enjoy a small portion of the money. She booked a trip to Italy, a destination she had always wanted to visit but had never been able to afford. It was a way to honor her uncle's memory, to celebrate the life he had lived and the gift he had given her.

As she worked through each step of her plan, Jasmine felt a growing sense of empowerment. She was making decisions that aligned with her values, that balanced her immediate desires with her long-term goals. The windfall was no longer a source of anxiety; it was an opportunity, a tool she could use to build the life she wanted.

The months that followed were transformative for Jasmine. The financial security she had gained allowed her to focus on other aspects of her life, her career, her relationships, her personal growth. Without the burden of debt, she felt freer, more in control of her future.

Jasmine also found herself becoming more financially savvy. She continued to meet with Karen regularly, discussing her investments and making adjustments as needed. She educated herself on personal finance, reading books and attending seminars to deepen her understanding of how to manage her money more effectively.

The windfall had been a turning point, not just financially, but in every aspect of her life. It had given her the confidence to take risks, to pursue opportunities she might have otherwise shied away from. She even began exploring the idea of starting her own business, a dream she always had but had never felt financially stable enough to pursue.

One day, as Jasmine was going over her finances, she realized just how far she had come. The investments she made were growing steadily, her emergency fund was secure, and she was well on her way to saving enough for a down payment on a house.

But more than that, Jasmine realized that the windfall had given her something far more valuable than money, it had given her the ability to make choices, to design her life in a way that reflected her values and aspirations.

She had taken a potentially overwhelming situation and turned it into an opportunity for growth and empowerment. And in doing so, she honored her uncle's memory in the best way possible, by using his gift to build a life of meaning and purpose.

Leveraging the Win-When Concepts

Jasmine's journey of managing her financial windfall exemplifies the principles of the Win-When approach in a powerful and transformative way. Faced with the sudden influx of a large sum of money, Jasmine didn't rush into spending it on immediate gratifications. Instead, she carefully evaluated her options, seeking guidance and creating a plan that aligned with both her current needs and long-term goals.

The Win-When philosophy emphasizes the importance of making decisions that ensure both present and future success. For Jasmine, this meant striking a balance between enjoying a portion of the windfall and then investing most of it in ways that would secure her financial future. By choosing to pay off her debts, establish an emergency fund, invest in a diversified portfolio, and save for a down payment on a house, she positioned herself for sustained financial stability.

Jasmine also demonstrated personal accountability, a key aspect of the Win-When mindset. She took ownership of her financial situation, sought advice from her financial advisor, and made deliberate choices that reflected her values and aspirations. Her willingness to invest most of the windfall, while still allowing herself to enjoy a portion of it, shows a mature and balanced approach to managing her finances.

Throughout her journey, Jasmine remained focused on the bigger picture. She understood that the windfall wasn't just about immediate gains; it was about creating a foundation for her future. By applying the Win-When principles, she was able to navigate a potentially overwhelming situation in a way that honored her values and set her up for long-term success.

In the end, Jasmine's story serves as a powerful reminder that financial success isn't just about having money, it's about making thoughtful, strategic decisions that align with one's goals and values.

Be True to Thyself

*"If you can't be true to yourself,
who can you be true to?"*

Marcus Blake sat in the sleek conference room; the Los Angeles skyline visible through the floor-to-ceiling windows behind him. The room was quiet, save for the soft hum of the air conditioning and the occasional rustle of paper. Across the table, the company's CEO, David Thompson, was wrapping up his pitch, a lucrative project that had the potential to skyrocket Marcus's career.

The offer was tempting. The project was high-profile, involving a major international client and a budget that would make any executive's eyes light up. It was the kind of opportunity that could lead to significant financial gain and further elevate Marcus's already successful career as a senior consultant at the firm.

But as David outlined the project's details, Marcus felt a growing unease. The project, while financially rewarding, required working with a client whose business practices were

155

questionable at best. There were ethical concerns, rumors of labor exploitation and environmental harm. Marcus had always prided himself on his integrity, and the thought of aligning himself with a company that disregarded such values didn't sit well with him.

David finished his pitch and leaned back in his chair, smiling confidently. "So, what do you think, Marcus? This is a huge opportunity. You're the perfect fit for this project, and I know you'll knock it out of the park."

Marcus hesitated, his mind racing. The financial rewards were undeniable, and the project could open doors to even bigger opportunities within the company. But at what cost? He had built his career on a foundation of integrity, choosing projects that aligned with his personal values and long-term goals. Taking on this project felt like a betrayal of everything he stood for.

As the silence stretched on, Marcus made up his mind. He couldn't accept the offer, not if it meant compromising his principles.

The Decision

"David, I appreciate the offer," Marcus began, choosing his words carefully. "This is exactly the kind of high-impact project I've been aiming for, and I'm honored that you see me as the right person to lead it."

David's smile widened, but Marcus wasn't finished.

"However," Marcus continued, his voice steady and strong, "I have to be honest with you. While the financial and professional opportunities are significant, I have concerns about the client's business practices. I've always believed that our work should reflect our values, and I'm not comfortable taking on a project that conflicts with those values."

David's expression shifted, the smile fading into a thoughtful frown. "I understand where you're coming from, Marcus, but this is business. Sometimes we have to make tough choices to achieve success."

"I agree," Marcus said, nodding. "But I also believe that true success isn't just about the bottom line. It's about aligning our work with our principles and contributing to something we can be proud of. I'm committed to this company and to my career, but I can't compromise on this. So, while I appreciate the offer, I must decline."

David looked at Marcus for a long moment, his expression unreadable. Finally, he nodded. "I respect your decision, Marcus. It's not often we see someone willing to turn down an opportunity like this because of their values. I'll find someone else for the project."

Marcus felt a wave of relief and a sense of pride in his decision. He had stood by his principles, even when it wasn't the easiest choice. But as he left the conference room, he couldn't help but wonder what the consequences would be. Would turning down the project affect his standing in the company? Would he miss out on future opportunities because of this decision?

The Aftermath

In the days that followed, Marcus continued with his usual workload, trying to push any doubts from his mind. He knew he had made the right decision, but the nagging thought of what he might have given up lingered in the back of his mind.

However, to his surprise, the atmosphere around him didn't shift negatively. In fact, several colleagues, having heard about his decision, surprisingly approached him with words of support.

"Marcus, I heard you turned down that big project," one of his peers, Lila, said as they passed each other in the hallway. "I have to say, I respect you even more for that. It's not easy to stand up for what you believe in, especially when there's a lot on the line."

"Thanks, Lila," Marcus replied, feeling a sense of affirmation. "It wasn't an easy decision, but it felt like the right one."

He received similar comments from others, and soon, it became clear that his choice had not gone unnoticed by the higher-ups either. A week later, Marcus was called into a meeting with the company's COO, Angela Mills.

Angela was known for her sharp business acumen and her commitment to corporate social responsibility, a value that resonated deeply with Marcus. As he entered her office, Angela greeted him with a warm smile.

"Marcus, thank you for coming in," she said, motioning for him to take a seat. "I've been hearing a lot about your decision regarding the recent project offer."

Marcus braced himself, unsure of where this conversation was headed. "Yes, I felt it was important to stick to my values, even though it was a difficult choice."

Angela nodded. "I admire that. It's not every day that someone turns down a lucrative opportunity because it doesn't align with their principles. That kind of integrity is exactly what we need more of in this company."

Marcus felt a flicker of hope. "Thank you, Angela. I was concerned about the impact of my decision, but it's reassuring to hear that it's appreciated."

"It's more than appreciated," Angela said, her tone serious. "It's the kind of leadership we need as we move forward. That's why I wanted to talk to you about a different opportunity, one that I believe aligns much more closely with your values and long-term career goals."

Marcus's interest was piqued. "I'm listening."

Angela leaned forward, her eyes alight with enthusiasm. "We're in the process of launching a new initiative focused on sustainable business practices and ethical consulting. It's a project that will require a leader who not only has a strong strategic mind but also a deep commitment to social responsibility. I think you'd be the perfect fit to head this initiative."

Marcus felt a rush of excitement. This was exactly the kind of work he had always wanted to do, using his skills to make a positive impact, not just for the company, but for the broader community.

"This sounds incredible," Marcus said, his voice filled with energy. "It aligns perfectly with what I believe in and where I see my career heading. I'd love to be part of this."

Angela smiled. "I had a feeling you'd say that. Let's discuss the details and see how we can make this work."

The New Opportunity

The weeks that followed were some of the most exhilarating of Marcus's career. Leading the new initiative on sustainable business practices was challenging, but it was also deeply fulfilling. He was able to use his expertise to drive real change within the company, implementing policies that promoted ethical behavior and sustainability across all departments.

The project wasn't just about meeting the company's goals, it was about setting a standard in the industry. Marcus found himself working closely with a team of like-minded individuals who shared his passion for social responsibility. They worked together to develop strategies that not only improved the company's reputation but also made tangible impacts on the communities they served.

One of the highlights of the project was a partnership with a nonprofit organization focused on environmental conservation. Through this partnership, Marcus's team was able to launch a series of initiatives that reduced the company's carbon footprint and supported sustainable practices in local communities. The project garnered positive attention both within the company and in the media, and Marcus's leadership was widely recognized as a driving force behind its success.

But the rewards weren't just professional. Marcus found that his work on the initiative brought him a deep sense of personal fulfillment. Every day, he knew that the decisions he made were aligned with his values, and that he was contributing to something meaningful.

As the initiative gained momentum, Marcus reflected on how far he had come since turning down the original project. The decision to stick to his principles led him to an opportunity that was aligned with his values and was also more impactful than anything he had done before.

Recognition and Growth

As the first year of the initiative came to a close, Marcus was invited to present the results at the company's annual leadership conference. It was a moment of pride for him, standing in front of his colleagues and senior executives, sharing the achievements of the project he led.

The presentation was met with enthusiastic applause, and afterward, Marcus was approached by several executives who praised his work.

"Marcus, this is exactly the kind of innovation and leadership we need," said one of the senior VPs. "You've set a new standard for how we approach our business, and it's having a ripple effect across the company."

Angela also pulled Marcus aside after the presentation. "You've done an outstanding job, Marcus. The success of this initiative is a demonstration of your leadership and your commitment to our values. We're already seeing the positive impact, and I'm confident this is just the beginning."

Marcus felt a deep sense of satisfaction. He had taken a risk by turning down the original project, but it paid off in ways he hadn't imagined. Not only had he found a way to align his work with his values, but he had also positioned himself as a leader within the company, someone who could successfully drive meaningful change.

But more than the recognition, it was the knowledge that he had stayed true to himself that mattered most. Marcus knew that the work he was doing was not only advancing his career but also making a difference in the world. It was a powerful reminder that success doesn't have to come at the expense of one's values, in fact, true success is often rooted in them.

Leveraging the Win-When Concepts

Marcus's journey of turning down a high-paying project and finding a better opportunity that aligned with his values is a powerful example of the Win-When concepts in action. Faced with a lucrative project that conflicted with his personal values, Marcus didn't rush into a decision based solely on immediate financial gain. Instead, he carefully evaluated how the project aligned with his long-term goals and principles.

The Win-When philosophy emphasizes the importance of making decisions that ensure both present and future success as well as maintained alignment with your core values and goals. For Marcus, this meant recognizing that while the initial project offered significant financial rewards, it also posed a risk to his integrity and long-term satisfaction. By choosing to decline the project, he prioritized his values, which ultimately led to a more fulfilling and impactful opportunity.

Marcus also demonstrated personal accountability, another key aspect of the Win-When mindset. He took ownership of his decision, communicated it clearly and confidently, and remained open to new opportunities that aligned with his goals. His willingness to stand by his principles not only preserved his integrity but also positioned him for greater success within the company.

The eventual outcome, leading a project that aligned with his values and made a meaningful impact, reinforced the idea that success is not just about immediate gains, but about making decisions that resonate with one's core beliefs and contribute to long-term fulfillment.

In the end, Marcus's story serves as a testament to the power of thoughtful, value-driven decision-making. By applying the Win-When concepts, he was able to navigate a challenging situation in a way that honored his principles and led to greater success both professionally and personally.

As a result, Marcus later found a new, more fulfilling opportunity within the company that better aligned with his values and long-term goals. Not only did he preserve his integrity, but his leadership on the new initiative led to recognition, respect, and a stronger professional position.

As you consider your decisions and reflect on them, remember that the Win-When approach is not about quick wins or immediate satisfaction. It's about making choices that resonate with your core values, that keep you aligned with your long-term goals, and that ensure both short-term and sustained success.

The journey ahead is about making thoughtful, value-driven decisions and learning to trust yourself through the process. Continue reflecting on how the Win-When approach can guide your actions as we delve into more real-life examples of thoughtful decision-making in the upcoming chapters

.

Buy, Sell or Hold

"You have to consume the fruit that is bought, to access the seed that will grow you a tree."

For as long as Erica Morgan could remember, her father had instilled in her the importance of financial literacy. He was a practical man, someone who believed in planning for the future and making sound financial decisions. It was his guidance that led Erica to make her first investment in her early twenties, a significant sum in a promising tech stock.

At the time, it was a risky move. The tech sector was booming, but with it came volatility. Yet Erica's father had always encouraged her to think long-term. "Invest in what you believe in," he had told her, "and don't be swayed by short-term fluctuations."

So, she held on to the stock, watching as it experienced the ups and downs typical of the market. Over the years, it grew steadily, weathering economic downturns and emerging stronger each time. As the company behind the stock evolved into a tech giant, the value of Erica's investment soared.

Now, nearly fifteen years later, Erica found herself in a position she hadn't anticipated, deciding whether to sell the stock that had been her nest egg for so long. The stock had appreciated significantly, far beyond her initial expectations. Selling now would mean a substantial profit, a windfall that could change her life in meaningful ways.

But selling also meant letting go of something that had been a constant in her financial strategy. Her $5,000 investment in the stock had grown more than 35 times in value, and there was a strong argument to be made for holding on, given the company's continued growth potential. Yet, as Erica weighed the options, she couldn't ignore the other factor influencing her decision, the desire to purchase her first home.

For years, Erica had rented an apartment in the city, content with the flexibility it offered. But as she approached her late thirties, the idea of owning a home became more appealing. It wasn't just about having a place of her own; it was about stability, a place to put down roots and perhaps start a family.

The potential profit from selling the stock would provide the down payment she needed to buy a house in her dream neighborhood. But was it the right time to sell? Was she letting go of an investment with even more growth potential for something that, while valuable, might not offer the same financial return?

Seeking Advice

Erica knew she needed advice, and there was no one she trusted more than her father. They met for lunch at a quiet diner, a place they often went to when they needed to discuss important matters. As they settled into their seats, Erica explained her dilemma.

"Dad, I've been thinking about selling my stock," she began, sipping on her lemonade. "It's appreciated a lot, and I could use the money to buy a house. But part of me wonders if I should hold on a bit longer. The company's doing great, and there's still room for growth."

Her father listened intently, nodding as she spoke. "You've done an incredible job with that investment, Erica. It's not an easy decision to make, but I think it comes down to what your priorities are right now. What do you want more, a potentially bigger return down the road, or the stability and security of owning a home now?"

Erica sighed. "That's exactly what I've been struggling with. I want both, but I know I can't have it all. If I sell now, I'm giving up on the potential future gains. But if I don't, I'm delaying something I really want."

Her father leaned forward, his expression as a caring parent. "Here's the thing, no one can predict the market with absolute certainty. The stock could continue to grow, or it could face a downturn. But you've always been strategic about your investments, and you've set a target price for this one. The question is whether selling now aligns with your overall financial goals."

Erica nodded, understanding what he was getting at. "It does, actually. I've always wanted to own a home, and this is the first time I've felt financially ready to do it. But it's still hard to let go of something that's been such a big part of my financial journey."

Her father smiled. "That's understandable. But remember, investing is about making choices that align with your goals at different stages of your life. If buying a home is what you want, and the stock has reached the target price you set, then maybe it's time to take that step. You're not losing anything, you're just shifting your investment into something that brings value in a different way."

Erica felt a sense of clarity wash over her. Her father was right, this wasn't just about the potential financial gain. It was about aligning her decisions with her current priorities and long-term goals.

The Decision

Over the next few days, Erica spent a lot of time reflecting on her conversation with her father. She reviewed her financial strategy, considering how the sale of the stock would fit into her broader goals. The idea of owning a home, of having a place to call her own, grew increasingly appealing. It wasn't just about the financial aspect; it was about creating a stable foundation for the future.

She also considered the stock itself. The company had been a solid performer, but the tech market was unpredictable. Holding on to the stock could lead to further gains, but it could also expose her to greater risk if the market took a downturn.

Erica had always been a cautious investor, and she had set a target price for the stock years ago—one that it had now exceeded. Selling at this point would allow her to capitalize on the gains she has already made and invest in something that would bring her immediate and long-term benefits.

After much deliberation, Erica made her decision. She would sell the stock and use the proceeds to buy a home. It was the right choice for her at this stage in her life, one that aligned with both her financial strategy and her personal goals.

With her decision made, Erica contacted her financial advisor to discuss the logistics of selling the stock. They reviewed her investment portfolio, ensuring that the sale would not disrupt her overall financial plan.

"I've decided to sell it because it aligns with my investment strategy and long-term financial goals," Erica explained to her advisor. "I can use the returns now to invest in a home that will bring far more benefits now and in the future. And the rest I can move to stocks that are currently undervalued with the promise of good returns."

Her advisor nodded in agreement. "That sounds like a well-thought-out decision, Erica. You've done an excellent job with this investment and using the proceeds to buy a home is a smart move. Let's make it happen."

The Transition

With the decision made and the process underway, Erica felt a sense of relief and excitement. After the sale of the stock, she found herself with a substantial sum of money, more than enough for a down payment on a house in her dream neighborhood.

Erica spent the next few weeks house hunting, a process that was both exhilarating and nerve-wracking. She toured several properties, weighing the pros and cons of each one. But when she found the perfect house, a charming, sunlit home on a quiet street with a backyard and room to grow, she knew it was the one.

The home was everything she had hoped for, a place where she could see herself building a life. It was close to work, in a community she loved, and had all the features she wanted. Most importantly, it felt like a home, a place where she could put down roots and create lasting memories.

Erica made an offer on the house, and after a brief negotiation, it was accepted. The excitement of owning her first home was overwhelming, and she couldn't wait to move in and make it her own.

The day of the closing finally arrived. Erica signed the papers and felt a deep sense of accomplishment. She had made a smart investment all those years ago, and now, that investment was providing her with the means to achieve another important goal. It was a full-circle moment, one that validated her decision to sell the stock.

Moving into her new home was a whirlwind of activity, but Erica relished every moment. She spent hours decorating, choosing colors and furnishings that reflected her style and personality. Each room was a canvas, and she took her time creating spaces that were both beautiful and functional.

As she settled into her new life as a homeowner, Erica reflected on the journey that had brought her here. The decision to sell the stock hadn't been easy, but it had been the right one. The financial security it provided allowed her to take this important step, and the home itself brought her a sense of stability and fulfillment that went beyond any financial gain.

Owning a home also opened up new opportunities for Erica. She hosted friends and family for dinner parties, celebrated holidays in her own space, and even started a small garden in the backyard, a long-held dream of hers. The house became a sanctuary, a place where she could relax, recharge, and build the life she wanted.

Financially, Erica remained diligent. She continued to invest, focusing on a diversified portfolio that included stocks, crypto, and real estate. The sale of her original investment had provided her with the means to diversify further, and she was careful to maintain a balanced approach to her finances.

But beyond the financial benefits, Erica found that the decision to buy a home had brought her a deeper sense of purpose. It was a tangible achievement, a reflection of her hard work, and a symbol of the stability she had always sought.

Leveraging the Win-When Concepts

Erica's decision to sell her long-term investment and purchase a home is a clear demonstration of the Win-When philosophy in action. Faced with the choice of holding onto a stock with potential future gains or selling to achieve a significant personal goal, Erica didn't rush into a decision. Instead, she carefully evaluated how the sale would align with her broader financial strategy and personal aspirations.

The Win-When philosophy emphasizes the importance of making decisions that create immediate and sustained success. For Erica, selling stock provided her with the financial means to purchase a home, a long-term goal that brought her stability and fulfillment. By aligning her decision with her current priorities, she was able to achieve a significant milestone without compromising her financial future.

Erica also demonstrated personal accountability, another key aspect of the Win-When mindset. She took ownership of her decision-making process, seeking advice from her father and her financial advisor, and ultimately making a choice that reflected her values and goals. Her willingness to let go of an investment that had served her well to pursue a new opportunity is evidence of her ability to adapt and evolve her financial strategy to benefit her now and in the future.

Throughout her journey, Erica remained focused on the bigger picture. She understood that success wasn't just about maximizing financial returns, it was about making decisions that enhanced her overall quality of life. By applying the Win-When principles, she was able to navigate a complex financial decision in a way that honored both her present needs and her long-term goals.

In the end, Erica's story is a powerful reminder that success is not just about accumulating wealth, but about making choices that align with one's values and aspirations. By leveraging the Win-When concepts, she was able to achieve a meaningful and fulfilling outcome that will benefit her for years to come.

Time to Reflect

"Yesterday's choices become today's wisdom if you're willing to reflect and grow."

In the past three chapters, we explored the journeys of Jasmine, Marcus, and Erica as they faced significant decisions in their personal and professional lives. Each story demonstrates how the Win-When approach isn't just about present and future success but also about making decisions that align with core values and long-term goals.

The Win-When philosophy emphasizes thoughtful, value-driven decision-making, ensuring that your choices are not only strategic but also meaningful. Let's recap their stories and reflect on how they applied this concept.

The Unexpected Gift

Jasmine Henderson unexpectedly inherited $500,000 from her Uncle Mike. While overwhelmed with gratitude, she also felt the weight of responsibility. Her first instinct was to spend it on immediate needs like paying off debts, buying a car, or even taking a vacation.

177

But Jasmine wanted to ensure that her uncle's gift created long-term stability, honoring his memory by making wise decisions.

After seeking advice from her financial advisor, Jasmine developed a balanced plan. She paid off her debts, set aside money for a house down payment, created an emergency fund, and invested in a diversified portfolio. Importantly, she allowed herself to enjoy a small portion of the windfall by booking a long-dreamed-of trip to Italy.

Jasmine's story highlights how the Win-When approach encourages both present enjoyment and future security. By seeking guidance and considering her long-term goals, she avoided impulsive decisions and set herself up for sustained success. Jasmine's ability to align her financial decisions with her values, securing her future while allowing room for joy. was key to her journey.

Would you have managed such a windfall the same way?

How do you balance immediate desires with long-term planning in your own life?

Be True to Thyself

Marcus Blake, a successful senior consultant, was offered a high-profile project that promised major financial rewards and career advancement. However, the client involved had questionable business practices, raising ethical concerns for Marcus. Despite the potential for a significant career boost, Marcus couldn't ignore the conflict between his personal values and the nature of the project.

After careful reflection, Marcus declined the offer, prioritizing his integrity over the immediate gains. While initially uncertain about the repercussions of his decision, he soon found that his leadership was admired.

His ethical stance earned him a new opportunity, leading a corporate initiative focused on sustainable business practices, a role that perfectly aligned with his values and long-term goals.

Marcus's story exemplifies the Win-When principle that success is not merely about financial gains or climbing the corporate ladder, it's about staying true to your values. By turning down a project that conflicted with his principles, Marcus made room for an opportunity that brought him fulfillment and recognition in the company.

Would you have made the same choice as Marcus, or would the financial gain have tempted you to compromise?

How often do your decisions align with your personal values?

Buy, Sell, or Hold

Erica Morgan had been holding on to a tech stock for 15 years, watching it grow more than 35 times in value. While the stock had the potential to keep growing, Erica was faced with a new priority, buying her first home. Selling the stock would give her the financial means to achieve that goal, but she feared losing out on future gains if she cashed out too soon.

After consulting with her father and financial advisor, Erica decided to sell the stock. She used the proceeds for a down payment on her dream home while ensuring her financial future by diversifying her investments. The decision allowed her to fulfill her personal goal of homeownership, while still safeguarding her financial future.

Erica's journey shows how the Win-When approach involves making decisions that not only benefit you financially but also enhance your quality of life. By aligning her investment strategy with her current priorities, homeownership and long-term stability, she achieved both financial and personal success.

Would you have held onto the stock in hopes of greater financial rewards, or would you have prioritized the purchase of a home?

How do you balance financial decisions with personal goals?

The Win-When approach is not about chasing quick wins or momentary satisfaction. Instead, it's about aligning your decisions with your core values and goals, ensuring that each choice contributes to both immediate success and long-term fulfillment. In each of these stories, Jasmine, Marcus, and Erica faced different challenges, but they all made decisions that balanced their present needs with their aspirations for the future.

As you reflect on these stories, take a moment to consider your own decision-making process.

How often do you evaluate whether your choices are in line with your values and long-term goals?

Are you focused on making decisions that not only offer success today but also position you for sustained success in the future?

The Win-When journey is about trusting yourself, making thoughtful choices, and committing yourself to a life that honors what matters most to you. As we move forward, continue to reflect on how these principles can guide you toward more meaningful and sustainable success in your personal and professional life.

In the upcoming chapters of It's a Win-When, we will explore how the Win-When approach can guide you through complex decisions where values, emotions, and long-term goals intersect each other.

We'll tackle workplace conflict with your manager and another scenario with a co-worker. In either case, should you speak up or hold your peace? Go to HR? Confront them directly? We'll discuss how to resolve such conflicts while upholding your values and ensuring team cohesion.

We'll dive into the personal decision of when to start a family. How do you balance your professional growth with your desire to have children?

We also look at a couple of examples of how to deal with problems between friends. After falling out with a close friend, you're unsure whether to confront the issue or let it pass, and friends who have issues and how to help them.

How do you decide if the friendship is worth salvaging, and how can you approach the situation with empathy while maintaining your boundaries?

These upcoming chapters will demonstrate how the Win-When approach helps you make thoughtful, value-driven decisions. As we delve into these scenarios, reflect on your own experiences and consider how this approach can bring clarity to your decision-making process in your personal life.

You Could Cut It
With a Knife

*"What do you do when the problem
asks you what the problem is?"*

Nathan Carter had always prided himself on being a team player. As a project manager at a well-respected tech company, he had built a reputation for his calm demeanor, his ability to solve problems, and his skill in bringing out the best in his team. He enjoyed the collaborative environment of his workplace, where people were encouraged to share ideas and work together to achieve their goals.

But lately, things have changed.

The shift began when Sandra Mitchell was brought on as the new department head. Sandra was an experienced professional with a track record of success, but she was also known for her abrasive style. From the moment she took over, her loud and domineering presence was impossible to ignore. Her criticism, often harsh and unconstructive, was delivered in a tone that left little room for discussion. It wasn't long before the once-harmonious team dynamics began to fray.

Nathan had always believed in the power of constructive feedback, the kind that helped people grow and improve. But Sandra's approach was the opposite. She was quick to point out mistakes, often in front of others, and her comments were more cutting than helpful. Nathan had tried to brush it off at first, telling himself that it was just her way of pushing the team to be better. But as the weeks went on, the situation only worsened.

One afternoon, during a meeting to discuss the progress of a critical project, Sandra's behavior reached a new low. The team was reviewing the latest milestones when Sandra interrupted Nathan mid-sentence.

"This is unacceptable," she snapped, her voice ringing out across the room. "We're behind schedule, and this is not the quality of work I expect from this team. Nathan, I don't know what you're doing, but you need to get it together."

Nathan felt his face flush with embarrassment and anger. He had been working tirelessly to keep the project on track, but the constant barrage of criticism was wearing him down. The rest of the team looked uncomfortable, shifting in their seats, clearly feeling the tension.

Sandra continued, her voice growing louder. "If you can't handle this, maybe we need to find someone who can."

The words stung, but Nathan kept his composure. He knew that responding in kind would only escalate the situation. But something had to change, this was no way to lead a team, and the toxic atmosphere was beginning to affect everyone's performance.

The Breaking Point

After the meeting, Nathan returned to his office, his mind racing. He knew he couldn't continue working under these conditions, but confronting Sandra felt like a risky move. She was his boss, after all, and challenging her could have serious repercussions for his career.

But the more he thought about it, the more he realized that something had to be done. Sandra's behavior wasn't just affecting him; it was affecting the entire team. Productivity was down, morale was at an all-time low, and people were beginning to dread coming to work.

Nathan decided to reach out to a trusted colleague, Olivia, who had been with the

185

company for years and had seen her fair share of difficult situations.

"Olivia, can I talk to you about something?" Nathan asked, knocking on her office door.

"Of course," Olivia replied, gesturing for him to come in. "What's on your mind?"

Nathan explained the situation, detailing Sandra's behavior and how it was impacting the team. He spoke about the constant criticism, the public reprimands, and the growing tension in the office.

Olivia listened carefully, nodding as Nathan spoke. "I've noticed it too," she said when he finished. "Sandra's approach is definitely causing problems. But confronting her directly could be tricky. Have you thought about how you want to handle it?"

Nathan sighed. "That's the thing, I'm not sure how to approach her without making things worse. But I also can't just sit back and let this continue. It's affecting everyone, and I feel like I need to do something."

Olivia leaned back in her chair, thinking. "You're in a tough spot, Nathan. But I think the key is to approach it from a place of collaboration, not confrontation. If you go in guns blazing, it's likely to backfire. But if you frame it as a discussion about how to improve the team's performance and work more effectively together, she might be more receptive."

Nathan nodded, taking her advice. "That makes sense. I want to keep it professional and focused on the work, not make it personal."

"Exactly," Olivia said. "And make sure to emphasize that you value her leadership and want to find ways to support her goals. If you can make her see that you're on the same team, it might help diffuse the tension."

Nathan left Olivia's office feeling a bit more prepared, but still nervous. The thought of confronting Sandra was daunting, but he knew it was the right thing to do. He just hoped it wouldn't backfire.

The Conversation

The next day, Nathan gathered his thoughts and drafted an email to Sandra, requesting a one-on-one meeting. He kept the tone respectful and professional, emphasizing that he wanted to discuss how they could work together more effectively to achieve the team's goals.

Sandra responded quickly, agreeing to meet later that afternoon. As the time approached,

Nathan felt his nerves building, but he reminded himself of what Olivia had said, this was about collaboration, not confrontation.

When he arrived at Sandra's office, she greeted him with her usual brusque demeanor. "Alright, Nathan, what's this about?"

Nathan took a deep breath, choosing his words carefully. "Sandra, I wanted to talk to you about the project and how we're working together as a team. I really value your leadership, and I think we all want to make sure we deliver the best results possible. But I've noticed that there's been some tension lately, and I think it's affecting our productivity."

Sandra raised an eyebrow. "Tension? What kind of tension?"

"It seems like there's been a lot of stress and frustration on the team," Nathan explained. "I think some of it comes from how feedback is being delivered. I know we're all under pressure to meet our deadlines, but I've noticed that the way criticism is communicated can sometimes be more disruptive than constructive. It's affecting morale, and I'm concerned it's impacting our work."

Sandra's expression hardened slightly. "Are you saying I'm the problem?"

Nathan shook his head. "Not at all. I'm saying that we all want to improve, and I think we could benefit from finding a way to give feedback that's more focused on solutions and less on pointing out mistakes. I want to support you in leading this project, and I think the team would respond better to a more collaborative approach."

For a moment, there was silence. Nathan could feel his heart pounding, unsure of how Sandra would react.

Finally, she spoke, her tone measured. "I see what you're saying, Nathan. I can be direct, and I know that sometimes comes across as harsh. But I'm trying to push the team to be better, and I don't have time for coddling."

"I understand that," Nathan said. "And I think we all appreciate that you want us to excel. But I believe we can find a balance, where we're still pushing for excellence, but in a way that builds people up rather than tearing them down. I think it would help the team perform better and feel more confident in their work."

Sandra leaned back in her chair, considering his words. "Alright, Nathan. I'll think about what you've said. But I expect results. If we're going to do this your way, I need to see that it's working."

"Of course," Nathan agreed. "I'm committed to making this project a success, and I'm here to support you in any way I can."

In the days that followed, Nathan noticed a subtle but significant shift in Sandra's behavior. She was still demanding, but her tone was less harsh, and she began to give feedback that was more constructive. When she pointed out issues, she also offered suggestions for how to address them, rather than simply criticizing them.

The change wasn't drastic, and Sandra was still very much the strong-willed leader she had always been. But the atmosphere in the office began to improve. The team seemed more relaxed, more willing to share ideas and take risks without fear of being publicly reprimanded.

Nathan continued to work closely with Sandra, making an effort to reinforce the positive changes. He praised her when she offered constructive feedback, and he made sure to highlight the team's successes, no matter how small. Gradually, the tension that had once permeated the office began to dissipate.

One afternoon, as the team was wrapping up a particularly challenging project milestone, Sandra called Nathan into her office.

"Nathan, I wanted to thank you for our conversation the other day," she said, her tone uncharacteristically sincere. "I've been trying to be more mindful of how I communicate with the team, and I've noticed a difference. I think it's helping, and I appreciate you bringing it to my attention."

Nathan smiled, feeling a sense of relief and accomplishment. "I'm really glad to hear that, Sandra. I think the team is responding well, and it's made a big difference in how we're working together."

Sandra nodded. "I'm not saying I'm going to change completely; I am who I am. But I see the value in what you were saying, and I'm willing to keep working on it."

Nathan felt a weight lift off his shoulders. The situation wasn't perfect, but it was a vast improvement from where they had started. He had taken a risk by addressing the issue, but it had paid off in a better working environment for everyone.

The Long-Term Impact

As the months went on, the improvements in the office culture continued. The team became

191

more cohesive, and their productivity increased. People were more willing to collaborate, to share ideas, and to take initiative without fear of harsh criticism.

Sandra's leadership style remained firm, but it was tempered with a newfound awareness of how her words and actions affected those around her. She still demanded excellence, but she did so in a way that encouraged growth rather than instilling fear.

Nathan's relationship with Sandra also improved. They developed a mutual respect, and Sandra began to rely on Nathan as a sounding board for her ideas. She appreciated his perspective and often sought his input before making decisions that would impact the team.

The changes weren't just limited to the office. Nathan found that his experience dealing with Sandra had made him a more confident and assertive leader. He had learned how to navigate difficult conversations with tact and professionalism, and it strengthened his ability to manage his team effectively.

One day, as Nathan was reflecting on the past year, he realized just how much the situation had taught him. He had faced a significant challenge, one that could have easily led to ongoing tension and a toxic work environment. But by addressing the issue head-on, with a focus on collaboration and constructive feedback, he had helped create a better workplace for everyone.

Leveraging the Win-When Concepts

Nathan's approach to dealing with a difficult colleague, particularly one in a position of authority, is a textbook example of the Win-When philosophy in action. Faced with a challenging situation that could have led to ongoing tension and a toxic work environment, Nathan didn't shy away from addressing the issue. Instead, he carefully considered the potential outcomes and chose a path that aligned with his long-term goal of creating a positive, productive workplace.

The Win-When philosophy emphasizes the importance of making decisions that ensure both immediate and sustained success. For Nathan, this meant addressing Sandra's behavior in a way that was constructive rather than confrontational. By framing the conversation as a discussion about how to improve the team's performance, Nathan was able to communicate his concerns without escalating the situation. This approach not only defused the immediate tension but also led to long-term improvements in the work environment.

Nathan also demonstrated personal accountability, a key aspect of the Win-When mindset. He took ownership of the situation, recognizing that his silence would only allow the problem to fester. By choosing to speak up, Nathan showed that he was committed to the well-being of the team and the success of the project. His willingness to engage in a difficult conversation, while maintaining respect and professionalism, ultimately led to a better working relationship with Sandra and a more positive atmosphere for everyone.

Throughout his journey, Nathan remained focused on the bigger picture. He understood that the goal wasn't just to avoid conflict, but to create an environment where the team could thrive. By applying the Win-When principles, Nathan was able to navigate a challenging situation in a way that honored his values and contributed to the long-term success of the team.

In the end, Nathan's story serves as a powerful reminder that difficult conversations, when handled with care and respect, can lead to positive change. By leveraging the Win-When concepts, Nathan was able to transform a potentially toxic situation into an opportunity for growth and improvement, benefiting not only himself but everyone around him.

Profits or Precious Moments

"Balancing a career and family is like walking a tightrope – sometimes you lean into the dream, and other times you lean into the love."

David Marshall had always been a man with a plan. At 32, he was well into his career as an underwriter in the insurance industry, steadily climbing the corporate ladder. He had worked hard to get where he was, often putting in long hours and sacrificing personal time to meet the demands of his job. It wasn't easy, but David knew that hard work and dedication were the keys to success in a competitive field.

However, as David sat at the dinner table one evening with his wife, Lisa, he found himself at a crossroads he hadn't fully anticipated. They had been married for four years, and the topic of starting a family had been a recurring theme in their conversations lately. Lisa was ready to take that next step, and while David shared her desire to start a family, he couldn't shake the feeling that the timing might not be right.

195

David's career was at a critical phase. He had recently been promoted to a senior underwriter position, a role that came with increased responsibilities and the potential for further advancement. His company had big plans for him, and David was eager to prove himself. The idea of taking on the additional responsibilities of fatherhood while trying to establish himself in this new role was daunting.

But there was more to the decision than just his career. David loved Lisa deeply, and he knew how much starting a family meant to her. He wanted to be there for her, to support her, and to share in the joy of raising a child. The thought of delaying their plans, of putting their family dreams on hold, weighed heavily on him.

As David and Lisa discussed the future, the conversation inevitably turned to the timing of starting a family.

"David, I know your career is important, and I support you 100%," Lisa said, her voice gentle but firm. "But I also don't want us to keep waiting for the perfect time. What if it never comes? We've built a great life together, and I think we're ready for this next step."

David nodded, his mind racing. He understood where Lisa was coming from, but he couldn't help but feel the pressure of his career ambitions. "I know, Lisa. I want to start a family too, but I'm worried about how we'll manage everything. My new role is demanding, and I don't want to shortchange you or our future child because I'm too focused on work."

Lisa reached across the table and took his hand. "We'll figure it out together. You're not in this alone, David. We've always been a team, and we can handle whatever comes our way."

David squeezed her hand, appreciating her support. But the decision wasn't any easier. He knew he needed to weigh his options carefully before making a choice that would affect both their lives.

Weighing the Options

The days following their conversation were filled with contemplation. David couldn't stop thinking about the potential outcomes of their decision. On the one hand, starting a family now would bring immediate fulfillment and joy. He could imagine the happiness of welcoming a child into their lives, the excitement of watching their family grow. It was a dream he had always envisioned for the future.

But on the other hand, David knew that starting a family could also strain his career progress. The insurance industry was highly competitive, and taking time away from work, even for paternity leave, could slow his momentum. There was also the concern of balancing the demands of his job with the responsibilities of fatherhood. Would he be able to give the attention they deserve?

David found himself constantly running through scenarios in his mind. What if he waited a few more years until he was more established in his career? By then, he might be in an even better position to provide for his family, with a more flexible schedule and greater financial security.

But what if they waited too long? Life was unpredictable, and there was no guarantee that the perfect time would ever come.

One evening, David decided to seek advice from someone who had been in a similar situation, his mentor, James Turner. James was a senior executive at the company, a man David respected not only for his professional achievements but also for his ability to balance work and family life.

"James, do you have a few minutes to chat?" David asked as he stepped into his mentor's office.

"Of course, David. What's on your mind?" James replied, looking up from his desk.

David hesitated for a moment before diving in. "Lisa and I have been talking about starting a family, but I'm struggling with the timing. My career is in a crucial phase, and I'm worried about how I'll manage everything if we have a child now. But at the same time, I don't want to keep delaying our plans for the sake of my career."

James nodded thoughtfully. "That's a tough decision, David. I've been there myself, and I know how challenging it can be to balance career ambitions with family life. But let me ask you this, what's most important to you right now?"

David considered the question carefully. "I want to succeed in my career, but I also want to start a family with Lisa. I don't want to choose one over the other, but I'm not sure how to make it all work."

James smiled. "It's natural to feel that way. But the truth is, there's rarely a perfect time to start a family. There will always be challenges, whether it's work, finances, or something else. What matters is whether you and Lisa feel ready for this next step and whether you're willing to make the necessary adjustments to balance both aspects of your life."

David listened intently, appreciating James's perspective. "So, you're saying it's possible to do both?"

"It's not only possible, David, but it's also rewarding," James replied. "It won't be easy, and there will be times when you'll need to prioritize one over the other. But with the right support and mindset, you can find a balance that works for you. The key is to communicate openly with Lisa and to be flexible in how you approach your career and family life."

David left the meeting with a renewed sense of clarity. He knew the decision wouldn't be easy, but he felt more confident in his ability to make the right choice.

The Decision

After much thought and discussion with Lisa, David knew it was time to make a decision. He reflected on everything he had learned from his conversations with Lisa and James, as well as his own internal deliberations.

David realized that while his career was important, it wasn't the only thing that mattered to him. The idea of starting a family brought him a sense of joy and fulfillment that no career achievement could match. He also recognized that waiting for the perfect moment could lead to endless delays and missed opportunities. Life was about balance, and he believed that with careful planning and support, he could manage both his career and a growing family.

One evening, as David and Lisa sat together on the couch, he took her hand and looked into her eyes. "Lisa, I've thought carefully about this decision, and I believe that starting a family now is the right choice for us. I'm committed to balancing both aspects of my life and ensuring that I can provide stability and support for our family while continuing to advance in my career."

Lisa's face lit up with a smile. "David, I'm so happy to hear that. I know it's a big decision, but I believe we can do this together."

David felt a sense of relief washing over him. The decision had been weighing on him for so long, but now that it was made, he felt more at peace. He knew there would be challenges ahead, but he was ready to face them with Lisa by his side.

The Journey Begins

With the decision made, David and Lisa began planning for the future. They discussed everything from finances to childcare to how they would manage their time once the baby arrived. David also spoke with his boss about his plans, ensuring that he would have the flexibility to take paternity leave and adjust his work schedule as needed.

At work, David continued to excel in his role as a senior underwriter. He found that the decision to start a family had given him a renewed sense of purpose and focus. Knowing that he was working to provide for his future family motivated him to perform at his best, and his colleagues noticed a positive change in his attitude.

As the months passed, Lisa became pregnant, and the reality of becoming a father began to sink in for David. He attended every doctor's appointment, helped Lisa prepare the nursery, and spent countless hours reading books about parenting and fatherhood. The more he learned, the more excited he became about the prospect of starting a family.

At the same time, David remained committed to his career. He continued to take on challenging projects, but he was careful not to overextend himself. He communicated openly with his colleagues and superiors about his plans, ensuring that he had the support he needed to balance his professional and personal responsibilities.

The birth of their daughter, Emma, was a life-changing moment for David. Holding her in his arms for the first time, he felt a rush of emotions, love, joy, responsibility, and a deep sense of gratitude. At that moment, he knew he had made the right decision. His career was important, but nothing could compare to the fulfillment of becoming a father.

Finding Balance

The months following Emma's birth were some of the most challenging and rewarding of David's life. He quickly learned that balancing the demands of fatherhood with his career required careful planning, flexibility, and a willingness to adapt.

David and Lisa worked together to create a routine that allowed them both to fulfill their professional responsibilities while caring for their daughter. David took on the early morning feeding so that Lisa could get some rest, and he made sure to be home in time for dinner and bedtime routines. He also arranged to work from home a few days a week, allowing him to spend more time with Emma while staying on top of his work.

There were days when the juggling act felt overwhelming, but David remained focused on his priorities. He reminded himself that this was a temporary phase, and that the effort he was putting into both his career and his family would pay off in the long run.

At work, David's commitment to balance earned him the respect of his colleagues and superiors. They saw that he was dedicated to his job, but also that he valued his family and was willing to make adjustments to ensure their well-being. His ability to manage both aspects of his life effectively became a model for others in the company, and he was often sought out for advice on work-life balance.

As Emma grew, David found that the joy of watching her develop and thrive far outweighed any challenges he faced in his career. He was present for her first steps, her first words, and all the milestones that made parenthood so rewarding. These moments reinforced his belief that he had made the right decision, and that the balance he had worked so hard to achieve was worth every effort.

The Long-Term Impact

As the years passed, David continued to build a successful career while being an active and involved father. He received several promotions and was eventually offered an executive position within the company. But no matter how demanding his career became, he never lost sight of what mattered most, his family.

David and Lisa had two more children, and their home was filled with love, laughter, and the occasional chaos that comes with raising a family. David made it a priority to be present for his children, attending school events, coaching their sports teams, and spending quality time with them on weekends.

Looking back, David realized that his decision to start a family when he did had been one of the best choices he had ever made. It hadn't been easy, and there were times when he had to make sacrifices and tough decisions to maintain the balance he valued so much. But the rewards had been immeasurable.

David's career continued to flourish, but he knew that his greatest achievement was the family he had built with Lisa. The love and support they shared had given him the strength to pursue his professional goals while being the father and husband he always wanted to be.

Leveraging the Win-When Concepts

David's decision to start a family while balancing a demanding career is a powerful example of the Win-When concepts in action. Faced with the challenge of choosing between immediate fulfillment and long-term career goals, David carefully evaluated his options and made a decision that aligned with both his personal and professional aspirations.

The Win-When philosophy emphasizes the importance of making decisions that ensure both present and future success. For David, this meant recognizing that starting a family would bring immediate joy and fulfillment, while also understanding that it would require careful planning and commitment to maintain his career trajectory. By choosing to start a family, David embraced the challenge of balancing both aspects of his life, knowing that it would require flexibility, communication, and support.

David also demonstrated personal accountability, a key aspect of the Win-When mindset. He took ownership of his decision, communicated openly with Lisa and his colleagues, and made deliberate choices to prioritize his family while continuing to advance in his career. His willingness to adapt and make sacrifices, when necessary, allowed him to achieve a balance that benefited both his professional and personal life.

Throughout his journey, David remained focused on the bigger picture. He understood that success wasn't just about achieving career milestones, but about creating a fulfilling and meaningful life that included both his professional goals and his role as a father and husband. By applying the Win-When principles, David was able to navigate the complexities of work-life balance in a way that honored his values and aspirations.

In the end, David's story serves as a powerful reminder that true success is about finding balance and making choices that align with what matters most. By leveraging the Win-When concepts, David was able to build a life that brought him both professional achievement and personal fulfillment, creating a legacy that will benefit his family for generations to come.

A Confrontation

"Don't let someone else's wrongdoings define your worth."

Brandon Simmons sat in his cubicle, his fingers hovering over the keyboard as he stared blankly at the screen. The hum of office chatter buzzed around him, but his mind was consumed by a problem that had been gnawing at him for weeks. His colleague, Marcus, had been undermining him at every turn. Not only was Marcus taking credit for Brandon's hard work, but he was also quick to blame him whenever something went wrong. The situation had grown intolerable, and Brandon's reputation within the company was starting to suffer.

Brandon had always prided himself on his professionalism and dedication. He had been with the company for five years, gradually working his way up from an entry-level position to a respected team leader in the product development department. His achievements spoke for themselves, or at least they used to. Recently, Marcus has found ways to subtly take credit for Brandon's successful projects, leaving Brandon's contributions largely unnoticed. Worse, whenever Marcus failed to meet his own deadlines or delivered subpar results, he shifted the blame onto Brandon, damaging his credibility.

This wasn't the first time Brandon had encountered difficult coworkers, but Marcus was different. His tactics were slick, and he played office politics with the precision of a master. Brandon had tried to ignore the behavior at first, hoping it would pass, but it hadn't. Now, his reputation and future opportunities at the company are at risk. He knew he had to do something, but what?

As Brandon sat there, he realized he needed a plan. He couldn't afford to make an impulsive decision, one that might backfire and make things worse. He had to approach this situation carefully, following a structured decision-making process to ensure that whatever action he took would align with his goals and preserve his integrity.

Define the Decision

Brandon knew the first step was to clearly define the decision he needed to make. It wasn't just about whether to confront Marcus or not. The decision was deeper than that, this was about protecting his reputation, maintaining a positive work environment, and ensuring his future career growth.

As he reflected on the situation, Brandon asked himself a few key questions:

- What is the specific decision I need to make?

- What problem am I addressing with this decision?

- What are the desired outcomes?

Brandon realized that the core issue was not just Marcus's behavior, but how it was affecting his reputation and future at the company. His decision wasn't just about whether to confront Marcus; it was about whether to take a stand to restore his credibility or continue to allow Marcus's behavior to undermine him. The desired outcome was clear: Brandon needed to ensure that his contributions were recognized, his reputation remained intact, and he wasn't blamed for Marcus's mistakes.

Gather Information

Next, Brandon knew he needed to gather as much information as possible about the situation. What was the company's culture around confrontation? How had others handled similar situations in the past? And most importantly, what kind of response could he expect from Marcus if he decided to confront him?

Brandon started by observing Marcus more closely. He paid attention to how Marcus interacted with others in the office, particularly when discussing projects or assigning credit. He noticed that Marcus had a pattern of speaking up during meetings just after Brandon shared a successful idea or presented results. Marcus would elaborate on Brandon's points, making it seem like the ideas were his own. When something went wrong, Marcus was quick to downplay his role and subtly suggest that Brandon had failed to deliver.

Brandon also spoke privately with a trusted colleague, Amanda, who had been with the company longer than he had. Amanda had dealt with difficult coworkers before and knew office politics well.

"Brandon, I've noticed what's been going on with Marcus," Amanda said one day over lunch. "You're not imagining it. He's taking credit for your work and shifting the blame on you when things don't go well. It's not right but confronting him could be tricky. He's well-connected with upper management, so you need to be strategic about how you handle this."

Brandon frowned, feeling the weight of Amanda's words. He hadn't realized just how well-connected Marcus was. "What do you think I should do? Should I confront him or just keep my head down?"

Amanda took a thoughtful sip of her coffee. "If you let this continue, it's only going to get worse. But you need to be careful about how you approach it. Document everything, your contributions, any instances where Marcus takes credit, and any mistakes he tries to pin on you. That way, if you do decide to confront him, you'll have evidence to back you up."

Brandon nodded. Amanda's advice made sense. He needed to gather concrete examples of Marcus's behavior before taking any action. That would allow him to approach the situation with facts, not just emotions.

Weigh the Options

With the information he had gathered, Brandon moved on to weighing his options. There were essentially two paths before him: he could confront Marcus and attempt to resolve the issue, or he could avoid confrontation and continue working under the shadow of Marcus's undermining behavior.

Option 1: Confront Marcus

- Pros: By addressing the issue head-on, Brandon could restore his reputation, make sure his contributions were recognized, and potentially gain Marcus's respect. If the confrontation went well, it could lead to better collaboration and a more positive work environment.

- Cons: Confronting Marcus could backfire. Marcus might react defensively, escalate the situation, or use his connections with upper management to paint Brandon as difficult to work with. The workplace atmosphere could worsen, making it harder for Brandon to succeed.

Option 2: Avoid Confrontation

- Pros: By avoiding confrontation, Brandon could maintain the status quo, keeping things relatively peaceful in the office. He wouldn't risk worsening his relationship with Marcus or jeopardizing his standing with upper management.

- Cons: If Brandon didn't confront Marcus, Marcus would likely continue to take credit for his work and blame

213

him for failures. Over time, Brandon's reputation could suffer even more, making it harder to advance in his career. The long-term consequences could be severe.

As Brandon weighed these options, he realized that the long-term risks of avoiding confrontation were too high. His reputation was already starting to suffer, and if he didn't take action, things would only get worse. However, he also knew that confronting Marcus had to be done carefully.

Aligning with Values and Goals

Brandon then took a step back and asked himself how each option aligned with his core values and long-term goals. He valued integrity, respect, and fairness in the workplace. He wanted to be recognized for his contributions, but he also valued maintaining a positive and collaborative work environment. His long-term goal was to advance in the company and eventually move into a leadership position.

By confronting Marcus, and addressing the issue, he could ensure that his work was recognized and that he wasn't unfairly blamed for mistakes. It also aligned with his long-term goal of career advancement. He couldn't achieve his goals if Marcus continued to undermine him.

On the other hand, avoiding confrontation conflicted with Brandon's values. It would mean allowing unfair behavior to continue, which went against his sense of integrity. It also didn't support his long-term goals, as his reputation would continue to suffer if he didn't take action.

Making the Decision

With everything carefully considered, Brandon made his decision. He would confront Marcus, but he would do so in a way that minimized the risk of escalation. He decided that the best approach would be to have a private, professional conversation with Marcus, laying out the facts and expressing his concerns calmly and directly.

The next day, Brandon approached Marcus at the end of the workday. "Hey, Marcus, do you have a few minutes to talk? There's something I'd like to discuss with you."

Marcus looked up from his computer, his expression neutral. "Sure, Brandon. What's on your mind?"

Brandon led Marcus into an empty conference room and closed the door. Taking a deep breath, he began, "I've noticed a few things

215

lately that I think we need to address. There have been instances where my contributions to projects haven't been recognized, and it seems like you're taking credit for some of the work I've done. At the same time, I've been blamed for things that weren't my responsibility. I value teamwork, and I want to make sure we're on the same page. If this continues, I'll have to escalate the issue. But before that, I'd like to discuss how we can work together more effectively moving forward."

Marcus's expression tightened, but he didn't interrupt. After a moment, he leaned back in his chair and said, "I didn't realize you felt that way, Brandon. I can see how it might have come across like that, but that wasn't my intention. Let's talk about how we can improve communication between us."

Brandon was relieved that Marcus hadn't immediately gone on the defensive. They spent the next twenty minutes discussing ways to improve collaboration, agreeing to be more transparent about their contributions in meetings and share credit where it was due.

Evaluate and Adjust

Over the next few weeks, Brandon paid close attention to how Marcus behaved. While things weren't perfect, there was a noticeable improvement. Marcus no longer took credit for Brandon's work, and there were fewer instances of blame-shifting. Brandon felt more confident in meetings, knowing that his contributions were being recognized.

However, Brandon continued to document his work and any interactions with Marcus, just in case things took a turn for the worse. He remained vigilant, ready to make further adjustments if necessary. By evaluating the impact of his decision and being open to making changes, Brandon ensured that the situation stayed manageable.

Leveraging the Win-When Concepts

Brandon's decision to confront Marcus was a perfect example of applying the Win-When decision-making process. At each step, he carefully considered his options, gathering information, weighing the pros and cons, and ensuring that his decision aligned with both his immediate needs and long-term goals.

Brandon didn't rush into action without first clarifying the real issue. He knew that this wasn't just about a one-time confrontation, it was about protecting his reputation and future career growth.

Brandon took the time to observe Marcus's behavior and seek advice from a trusted colleague, ensuring that he had a clear understanding of the situation before making a move.

By carefully considering the potential outcomes of confronting Marcus versus avoiding the issue, Brandon was able to make a decision that balanced both short-term and long-term consequences.

Brandon's decision to face Marcus was rooted in his values of integrity, fairness, and respect. It also aligned with his long-term goal of career advancement.

Armed with facts and a clear plan, Brandon approached the situation calmly and professionally, ensuring that the confrontation was productive rather than confrontational.

After his discussion with Marcus, Brandon continued to evaluate the situation, ready to make further adjustments if needed. This resilience allowed him to maintain control of the situation and protect his reputation.

By following the Win-When process, Brandon was able to resolve the issue with Marcus in a way that supported both his immediate needs and his long-term career goals. His story is a testament to the power of structured decision-making and the importance of aligning decisions with one's values and goals.

The Weight of Friendship

*"The best kind of help is the kind
that doesn't feel like help."*

Joanne Fisher sat on her couch, the dim light from a single lamp casting a soft glow in her living room. The once-warm cup of tea in her hands had long gone cold as she stared out the window, her thoughts racing. A gentle autumn breeze rustled the leaves outside, but inside, Joanne's mind was a storm of concern and uncertainty.

Her best friend, Rachel, had always been a pillar in her life, a confidante, a partner in adventures, and someone who had stood by her through the highs and lows of life. But over the past few months, Joanne had noticed a troubling shift in Rachel's behavior. She had become more withdrawn, unreliable, and prone to mood swings. Joanne had heard the whispers of concern from their mutual friends, but it wasn't until she began to see it herself that she started to worry.

At first, Joanne chalked it up to stress. Rachel had been going through a difficult period at work and in her personal life, but the warning signs became harder to ignore. There were more missed plans, strange excuses, and a noticeable change in Rachel's appearance. Joanne suspected that her friend might be struggling with something far more serious, an addiction. But how could she confront her with it? What if Rachel shut her out? What if their friendship crumbled under the weight of such a sensitive conversation?

Joanne knew that this wasn't a decision to be taken lightly. Addressing her concerns could lead to Rachel seeking help, but it could also drive a wedge between them. As much as she feared losing her friend, Joanne also feared what might happen if she said nothing at all. She took a deep breath and leaned back on the couch, knowing she needed to approach this with care, following a structured decision-making process that would guide her toward the best course of action.

Define the Decision

Joanne understood that the first step in making any decision was to clearly define what needed to be addressed. This wasn't just about having a difficult conversation with Rachel; it was about her friend's well-being and the potential impact on their relationship.

She asked herself the critical questions to clarify the situation:

- What is the specific decision I need to make?

- What problem am I trying to address?

- What are the desired outcomes?

The problem, Joanne realized, was that she suspected Rachel was struggling with addiction, and the decision she faced was whether to confront her friend about it. The desired outcome was to help Rachel seek professional help if she needed it, but the underlying fear was how this might affect their friendship. Would Rachel become defensive, deny the problem, or worse, cut Joanne out of her life entirely?

Joanne's heart ached at the thought, but she knew she couldn't ignore the signs. The decision was clear: should she encourage Rachel to seek help, or should she stay silent, hoping that Rachel would come to her own realization? With this understanding, Joanne knew she had defined the true nature of her dilemma.

Gather Information

With the decision clearly defined, Joanne knew the next step was to gather as much information as possible about the situation. This meant understanding addiction better, learning how to approach someone who might be struggling, and considering the potential outcomes of such a confrontation. She needed to be prepared, both emotionally and intellectually, for whatever came next.

Joanne spent the next few days researching addiction. She read articles, watched interviews, and even spoke to a counselor who specialized in addiction and recovery. What she learned was sobering, addiction could affect anyone, and the path to recovery was often fraught with challenges. Confronting someone about their addiction was a delicate process, and it had to be handled with empathy and care. The counselor had emphasized the importance of timing and approach, warning Joanne that pushing too hard could cause Rachel to shut down or become defensive.

Joanne also reached out to a friend, Emily, who had gone through a similar situation with a family member. "It was one of the hardest conversations I've ever had," Emily admitted during a coffee chat. "But I knew I couldn't stay silent. My brother was spiraling, and I had to take the risk of straining our relationship to get him the help he needed. It didn't happen overnight, but eventually, he did seek help. I'll never regret speaking up, even though it was painful at the time."

Joanne nodded thoughtfully, feeling a mixture of hope and fear. She wanted to help Rachel, but was Rachel ready to listen? Could she handle the truth? Armed with more information, Joanne felt a little more prepared but knew that the decision would still require careful thought.

Weigh the Options

Now that Joanne had gathered the necessary information, it was time to weigh her options carefully. She could either confront Rachel about her concerns, risking the potential fallout, or avoid the confrontation entirely, allowing Rachel to continue down a path that might be destructive.

Option 1: Confront Rachel

- **Pros**: By addressing the issue, Joanne might encourage Rachel to seek help. If Rachel acknowledged the problem and took steps toward recovery, it could strengthen their friendship and lead to Rachel's well-being. Joanne would also feel that she had done everything in her power to help her friend.

- **Cons**: The conversation could backfire. Rachel might become defensive or deny the issue, potentially leading to a strain or even the end of their friendship. The confrontation might also push Rachel further into isolation, making it harder for her to seek help.

Option 2: Avoid Confrontation

- **Pros**: By avoiding the issue, Joanne could maintain peace in their friendship. She wouldn't risk a fallout, and Rachel might come to her own realization in time. Their friendship wouldn't be strained by an uncomfortable conversation.

- **Cons**: Ignoring the signs of addiction could lead to far worse consequences for Rachel. Without intervention, Rachel might continue down a dangerous path, and Joanne would have to live with the guilt of not speaking up when her friend needed her most.

As Joanne weighed these options, the long-term risks of avoiding confrontation became clearer. If she stayed silent, Rachel might never seek help, and Joanne would have to live with the knowledge that she hadn't tried to intervene. On the other hand, confronting Rachel could lead to immediate tension, but it might also be the catalyst that pushed Rachel toward recovery.

Aligning with Values and Goals

Joanne knew that any decision she made had to align with her core values and long-term goals, both in her life and in her relationships. She valued honesty, empathy, and loyalty, and she believed in standing by the people she cared about, even when it was difficult. Her long-term goal was to see Rachel happy and healthy, living her life to the fullest without the burden of addiction weighing her down.

Encouraging Rachel to seek help aligned with Joanne's values of loyalty and honesty. She couldn't stand by and watch her friend suffer in silence, especially when there was a chance that speaking up could lead to Rachel's recovery. However, avoiding the conversation conflicted with those values. It would mean turning a blind eye to a problem she knew was there, something that didn't sit right with Joanne.

The choice became clearer as Joanne reflected on her values. She knew she had to have the conversation with Rachel, even if it was hard, because helping her friend was more important than maintaining temporary peace.

Making the Decision

With all the information and reflections in mind, Joanne made her decision. She would talk to Rachel, but she would approach the conversation with care and compassion. This wasn't about accusing or blaming; it was about expressing her concern and offering support. Joanne knew that she couldn't control Rachel's response, but she could control how she communicated her message.

The next day, Joanne invited Rachel over for a quiet afternoon together. They had planned to watch a movie, but Joanne's heart was pounding as she tried to figure out the right moment to bring up her concerns. As they sat on the couch, the movie playing in the background, Joanne turned to her friend.

"Rachel," she began softly, "there's something I've been wanting to talk to you about, and it's been on my mind for a while."

Rachel looked at her curiously but didn't say anything.

Joanne took a deep breath. "I care about you so much, and lately I've been worried. I've noticed some changes, and I just want to make sure you're okay. I think it might be a good idea to talk to someone who can help you. I'll be with you every step of the way, but I don't want to see you struggling alone."

For a moment, there was silence. Rachel's face tightened, and Joanne feared she had said too much. But then, Rachel's expression softened, and she let out a shaky breath. "You noticed, huh?" she whispered. "I didn't want anyone to know. It's been really hard, and I don't know how to fix it."

Joanne felt a wave of relief wash over her. Rachel wasn't angry or defensive, she was scared and uncertain, but she wasn't shutting Joanne out. "You don't have to fix it alone," Joanne said gently. "We can find someone to help. You don't have to carry this by yourself."

Rachel nodded, tears filling her eyes. "Okay," she said quietly. "Let's figure this out together."

Evaluate and Adjust

In the weeks that followed, Joanne stayed by Rachel's side as she took the first steps toward seeking help. It wasn't an easy journey—there were setbacks and moments of doubt—but Joanne was grateful that she had made the decision to speak up. By addressing the issue, Joanne had helped her friend begin the process of recovery, and their friendship had grown stronger as a result.

Joanne also took time to reflect on the decision she had made. She had followed a structured process, weighed the risks and rewards, and ensured that her actions aligned with her values. There were moments when she had doubted whether she was doing the right thing, but in the end, she knew that her decision had been the right one for both her and Rachel.

Leveraging the Win-When Concepts

Joanne's decision to confront Rachel about her suspected addiction illustrates the importance of following the "Win-When" decision-making process. By approaching the situation with care, Joanne was able to make a decision that balanced both immediate concerns and long-term goals.

She took the time to understand the core issue at hand, which wasn't just about having a difficult conversation but about helping her friend while preserving their relationship. She gathered the necessary information about addiction and how to approach someone who might be struggling, ensuring she was prepared for the potential outcomes.

Joanne carefully considered the risks and rewards of both confronting Rachel and avoiding the issue. She realized that avoiding the conversation could have long-term negative consequences, while addressing it might lead to Rachel seeking help.

Her decision aligned with her values of loyalty, honesty, and empathy. She wanted what was best for Rachel and knew that avoiding the issue wouldn't serve that goal.

Joanne made the decision to speak up, approaching the conversation with care and compassion. Her thoughtful communication helped Rachel open up rather than shutting down.

She continued to support Rachel throughout her recovery journey, evaluating how their friendship had evolved and adjusting her approach as needed.

In the end, Joanne's decision was a testament to the power of thoughtful, structured decision-making. By following the Win-When process, she was able to help her friend while maintaining a strong, supportive relationship. Joanne's story is a reminder that with care, empathy, and a clear process, even the most difficult decisions can lead to positive outcomes for both the present and future.

To Forgive or Not to Forgive

"To forgive is to set a prisoner free and discover that the prisoner was you."

Trey sat in his home office, his mind swirling with thoughts, disbelief, and frustration. The afternoon sun filtered through the blinds, casting soft shadows on the papers strewn across his desk. He had been staring at his laptop screen for over an hour, trying to process the betrayal that had just occurred. His friend, Jordan, had done the unthinkable.

Trey had recently started a social media marketing business, and with excitement running high, he had brought Jordan onboard to handle sales. Jordan wasn't a partner, but Trey trusted him with an important role, responsible for building relationships and closing deals with clients. The trust Trey had placed in him now felt shattered. Jordan had misused company money to buy clothes and personal items, lying about purchasing an office laptop. He had bought a cheap, low-quality model rather than the one Trey had specified, pocketing the difference for himself.

230

Trey had known Jordan for over 10 years, and they'd built a solid friendship. That trust made it easy for Trey to bring him into the business. But now, Trey was left feeling betrayed and unsure whether he could forgive Jordan or if their friendship, and business relationship, was permanently damaged.

Step 1: Define the Decision

The first step Trey knew he had to take was to clearly define what decision needed to be made. This was no simple issue; it wasn't just about money but about trust and betrayal in both a professional and personal relationship. The decision seemed to be about whether he should forgive Jordan for the betrayal, but when Trey thought more deeply, he realized it was about much more.

The decision wasn't simply about forgiving a friend for making a bad choice. It was about the long-term impact on their friendship and whether Jordan's actions had destroyed the foundation of trust they had built over the years.

Trey asked himself the key questions of the Win-When approach:

- What is the specific decision I need to make?

- What problem or opportunity am I addressing with this decision?

231

- What are the desired outcomes?

- Are there any underlying issues that need to be addressed first?

He realized that the underlying issue wasn't just about the misuse of money, it was about whether Jordan could be trusted moving forward. Trey didn't want to lose his friendship, but he also couldn't ignore the betrayal. Forgiving Jordan might restore their friendship, but it could also lead to more trust issues in the future. On the other hand, not forgiving him could mean the end of their friendship but would give Trey peace of mind in knowing that he didn't have to worry about Jordan's integrity.

Step 2: Gather Information

After defining the decision, Trey knew he needed more information. He needed to understand what had led Jordan to make such a poor choice and whether there was any remorse. It wasn't enough to assume that Jordan had done it out of greed or carelessness. They needed to hear from him directly before making any judgment.

Trey called Jordan and asked to meet in person. They agreed to sit down at a nearby coffee shop. As they sat across from each other, Trey could see the discomfort in Jordan's posture. He seemed to know that he had messed up, but Trey needed to hear it from him.

"Jordan, I trusted you to handle something important for the business," Trey said, his voice steady but firm. "I gave you money to get the laptop and supplies, and instead, you lied and used it for yourself. I need to understand why."

Jordan shifted uncomfortably in his seat, avoiding eye contact. "Trey, I messed up," he admitted, his voice low. "I don't really have a good excuse. I've been struggling with my finances lately, and when I had that money in my hands, I just... I made a selfish decision. I didn't think about how it would affect you or the business. I thought I could get away with it and make it right later, but I realize now that I really screwed up."

Trey took a deep breath, processing Jordan's words. There was remorse in his voice, but was it enough? Would Jordan really change, or was this just the beginning of a pattern of bad behavior? Trey still needed to weigh his options.

Step 3: Weigh the Options

Trey sat down that evening to weigh his options carefully. On one hand, Jordan had been a good friend for the past ten years and forgiving him might salvage their friendship. Jordan had shown genuine remorse, admitted his mistake and offered an apology. However, forgiveness didn't mean Trey could simply forget what had happened.

He made a list of potential outcomes:

- **Forgive Jordan**: This could restore their friendship and allow them to move past the issue, but it could also lead to future trust issues. Could Trey ever fully trust Jordan in business again, knowing that he had been dishonest and used company funds for personal gain?

- **End the friendship**: This would give Trey peace of mind and prevent future betrayals, but it would also mean losing someone he had considered a close friend. Was this mistake worth losing a friendship over?

Trey also had to consider his business. Jordan's actions had jeopardized his growing company, and Trey couldn't afford to let such behavior slide. Trust was essential in business, and Jordan had broken that trust. But should a single mistake define their entire relationship?

Step 4: Align with Values and Goals

As Trey reflected on the situation, he realized that any decision he made had to align with his core values. Trey valued honesty, trust, and integrity. In business, these values were non-negotiable, and they also applied to his personal relationships. Jordan's actions had violated those values, and Trey needed to consider whether he could continue a friendship without compromising his standards.

Trey also considered his long-term goals. His business was growing, and he couldn't afford to have people involved who didn't share his commitment to professionalism and ethics. He wanted to build a company based on trust and collaboration, and if Jordan couldn't be a part of that, then Trey needed to move on.

But there was also the value of forgiveness. Trey had always believed in giving people second chances, especially when they showed genuine remorse. Was this one mistake worth ending the friendship, or could they work through it?

After much thought, Trey decided that while he could forgive Jordan as a friend, he couldn't trust him in a business setting again. Forgiveness was about letting go of the personal hurt, but it didn't mean Jordan should be given the same responsibilities in the company.

Step 5: Make the Decision

The next morning, Trey called Jordan. It was time to make a decision.

235

"Jordan," Trey began, "I've thought a lot about what happened, and I want to be honest with you. I forgive you for what you did, but I can't continue working with you in the business. I need people I can trust completely, and right now, that trust has been broken."

Jordan didn't argue or try to defend himself. "I understand, Trey. I really do. I'm sorry for putting you in this position, and I'll pay you back for the money I took. I just hope we can stay friends."

Trey nodded, even though Jordan couldn't see him. "We can, but it's going to take time to rebuild trust. I value our friendship, but I can't let this happen again. You'll need to work to make things right, both with the money and with me."

Jordan agreed, and Trey felt a sense of closure. He had made a decision that balanced both forgiveness and accountability. While their business relationship was over, their friendship still had a chance to heal.

Step 6: Evaluate and Adjust

In the weeks that followed, Trey kept an eye on how things were progressing. Jordan repaid the money he owed, and their conversations gradually returned to the easy-going camaraderie they once shared. However, Trey remained cautious. While he had forgiven

Jordan, he knew that trust would take time to rebuild.

Trey also took the time to reevaluate his own decision-making process. Had he made the right call? Could he have handled things differently? As he reflected, he realized that his choice had been the best possible outcome for both his business and his friendship. He had upheld his values, protected his business, and allowed room for personal growth.

Trey understood that not all friendships could withstand betrayal, but in this case, forgiveness had been the right move. It allowed him to maintain his personal values while safeguarding his business from future harm.

Reflection on the Win-When Approach

Trey's decision to forgive Jordan while ending their business relationship exemplifies the core principles of the Win-When approach. He didn't rush to judgment or make an emotional decision in the heat of the moment. Instead, he took the time to gather information, weighed his options, and ensured that his final choice aligned with both his immediate needs and long-term goals.

By evaluating the situation through a structured decision-making process, Trey was able to balance forgiveness with accountability. He didn't allow Jordan's betrayal to damage his business or compromise his values. Instead, Trey found a solution that maintained the integrity of his company while giving his friendship a chance to heal over time.

Trey also demonstrated personal accountability throughout the process. He recognized that while Jordan had made a serious mistake, Trey had the power to decide how it would affect their relationship moving forward. He took responsibility for setting boundaries, ensuring that future interactions with Jordan would be based on trust and mutual respect.

In the end, Trey's story highlights the importance of making decisions that not only address the immediate problem but also set the stage for long-term success. By following the Win-When approach, Trey ensured that both his business and personal life could thrive without compromising his values or goals.

Sitting Tall
Does Not Work

*"Stand tall, even when the world
is pushing you down."*

Casandra sat at the kitchen table, the weight of the family invitation heavy in her hands. The invitation was to her cousin's wedding, a significant family event that everyone was expected to attend. The card shimmered under the soft light, but instead of excitement, Casandra felt an overwhelming sense of dread. She had been staring at the invitation for hours, her mind replaying the painful events from years before.

A few years ago, Casandra's mother had passed away, and in the painful aftermath of her death, a significant sum of money had gone missing. It wasn't long before whispers began circulating within the family, accusing Casandra of stealing the money. The accusation was a devastating blow. Casandra had been very close to her mother, and the idea that she would do something so dishonorable was beyond hurtful. Yet, three family members, her aunt, her cousin, and her brother, had conspired against her, spreading the lie that it was Casandra who had taken the money. Only Casandra and those three knew the truth: it was they who had stolen the money and manipulated the situation to make her the scapegoat.

The lie had fractured the family. Most of the relatives believed the story, leaving Casandra isolated and hurt. She hadn't spoken to many of them since, and the few family gatherings she attended were tense and uncomfortable. Now, with this wedding invitation in hand, Casandra found herself facing a difficult decision.

Should she go to the wedding and risk confronting her accusers?

Or should she stay away, avoiding the inevitable tension but further deepening the distance between herself and the rest of her family?

Step 1: Define the Decision

The first step Casandra knew she had to take was to define what decision she was truly making. Was this simply about attending the wedding, or was there a deeper issue at play? The more Casandra thought about it, the more she realized this wasn't just about the event, it was about whether she was ready to face her family and, more importantly, her accusers.

She asked herself the key questions from the Win-When process:

- What is the specific decision I need to make?

- What problem or opportunity am I addressing with this decision?

- What are the desired outcomes?

- Are there any underlying issues that need to be addressed first?

Casandra realized that the underlying issue wasn't just attending the wedding; it was about whether she was ready to confront the family members who had lied about her.

Could she attend the event without it turning into a confrontation?

And what about her children? It wasn't fair for them to miss out on family events because of her unresolved issues with a few relatives.

If she went, could she focus on her children and the wedding itself, or would the tension overshadow everything?

Step 2: Gather Information

Casandra knew she needed more information before making a decision. First, she reached out to her cousin, the bride. She wanted to understand how important her presence was at the wedding and whether her cousin was

241

aware of the tension between her and the other family members.

The conversation was brief but enlightening. Her cousin was delighted to hear from her and genuinely wanted her to be at the wedding. "I know things have been tough with the family, Cas," her cousin said, her voice gentle. "But it would mean so much to have you there. I don't want you to miss out because of old issues."

After hanging up the phone, Casandra felt a tug of obligation. She wanted to be there for her cousin, but she knew the potential for conflict was high. To gather more perspective, Casandra also spoke to her closest friend, Maya, who had been her support throughout the difficult years following her mother's passing.

"You're stronger than you think, Cas," Maya told her. "I know you've been avoiding them, and I get it. But this might be a chance for you to reclaim your place in the family. If you go in prepared, you can handle it. Just don't let them drag you down."

The conversation gave Casandra a clearer picture of her options, but the decision was still difficult. She had the information, but she needed to consider the long-term impact.

Step 3: Weigh the Options

Casandra sat down with a notepad and began to weigh her options. On one side, attending the wedding meant potentially facing her accusers and the awkwardness of being around relatives who believed she had stolen from her mother. But it also meant showing up for her cousin and ensuring her children maintained a connection with their extended family. It could also be a chance to begin healing, but that was uncertain.

On the other hand, not attending would save her from immediate stress and confrontation, but it would also reinforce the distance between her and her family. Her absence would be noticed, and it might even lead to further isolation. Would staying away protect her or only prolong the pain?

Casandra asked herself:

- What are the possible options available to me?

- What are the potential benefits and drawbacks of each option?

- How does each option align with my values and goals?

Step 4: Align with Values and Goals

Casandra's core values revolved around family, integrity, and her responsibility as a mother. She wanted her children to have a relationship with their family, and despite the lies that had been told, she still cared about the family unit. But her integrity also mattered. She couldn't go to the wedding and let her accusers continue to smear her name.

One of her long-term goals was to repair her relationship with her family, but only if it could be done with honesty. Casandra didn't want to pretend nothing had happened, but she also didn't want to air all the dirty laundry at her cousin's wedding.

Casandra knew that if she attended, it had to be on her terms. She would have to address the conflict in a way that protected her boundaries and allowed her to enjoy the event without stirring up drama.

Step 5: Make the Decision

After much reflection, Casandra decided she would attend the wedding, but only after setting clear boundaries with her accusers. She needed to make sure the day wasn't ruined by unnecessary conflict, and she wasn't going to allow them to talk behind her back any longer.

She called her aunt first. The conversation was tense, but Casandra was calm and clear.

"I want to be at the wedding," Casandra said, "but I need to make something clear. I'm going to be there for the family and for the kids, but I won't tolerate any more lies or whispers behind my back. If I hear anything, I'll reveal the truth about what really happened with the money. I have the proof. So, let's keep things civil."

Her aunt tried to deflect, but Casandra held firm. "I'm not looking for a fight," she said, "but don't light a fire if you don't want the smoke."

She repeated the same conversation with her cousin and brother. By the time the calls were done, Casandra felt a sense of relief. She had set her boundaries, and if anyone crossed them, she was prepared to stand up for herself.

Step 6: Evaluate and Adjust

The day of the wedding came, and Casandra attended with her children. She was nervous but also determined. The event went smoothly, and while there were a few awkward moments with her aunt, cousin, and brother, there was no major conflict. Casandra kept her distance from them but was able to enjoy the event, focusing on her children and her cousin's happiness.

In the weeks that followed, Casandra reflected on her decision. Attending the wedding had been the right choice. It allowed her to reconnect with other family members and be present for her children. It hadn't completely resolved the conflict, but it was a step toward healing. She felt empowered by the boundaries she set, and for the first time in years, she didn't feel weighed down by the accusations.

Reflection on the Win-When Approach

Casandra's decision to attend the wedding while addressing the conflict in advance is a clear example of how to apply the Win-When approach. She didn't rush into a decision out of fear or avoidance. Instead, she took the time to gather information, weigh her options, and align her choice with her core values and long-term goals.

By setting clear boundaries with her accusers, Casandra demonstrated the resilience and self-respect required to navigate a difficult situation without compromising her integrity. The Win-When process allowed her to find a path that honored both her desire for family connection and her need for personal respect.

This story also highlights the importance of balancing short-term discomfort with long-term well-being. While attending the wedding was emotionally challenging, Casandra knew that avoiding the event would only deepen the divide between her and her family. Her decision to go on her terms, set the stage for future healing while maintaining her dignity.

In the end, Casandra's story reminds us that making good decisions requires both emotional intelligence and a structured approach.

Embracing the Win-When Mindset

"Winning today is good, but winning today and tomorrow? That's the real victory."

As you reflect on the scenarios we've explored throughout this book, I encourage you to think deeply about how you might have approached them.

How would you have handled Alyssa's dilemma of choosing between career advancement at Pinnacle Corp and the comfort of work-life balance at Axis Innovations?

Would you have been able to set the right boundaries and ask the tough questions to ensure a decision that not only benefits you now but also sets you up for the future?

Or what about Emma's decision to leave a toxic relationship for the sake of her well-being and her daughter's safety?

Could you find the courage to prioritize your mental health and make such a difficult, life-altering choice?

248

In both Trey's and Casandra's stories, we see profound reflections on the complexities of forgiveness, accountability, and personal growth. Both individuals face situations where trust is broken and the decisions they make will shape their futures, personally and relationally. Their reflective journeys teach us the balance between holding others accountable and embracing forgiveness without compromising personal values.

For Trey, his dilemma centered around whether he should forgive his friend Jordan, who betrayed his trust in a business context or end their relationship. Trey's decision-making process revealed that forgiveness does not mean allowing the same access or responsibility in the future.

He forgave Jordan personally but chose to sever the professional connection, recognizing that his business required trust and integrity that Jordan had undermined. This approach honors both accountability and compassion, allowing room for personal healing without jeopardizing his long-term goals.

Casandra's story, on the other hand, revolves around family betrayal and whether she could face her accusers at her cousin's wedding. Her decision to attend the wedding, while setting firm boundaries with those who wronged her, reflects her strength and resolve. She chose to protect her children's connection to the family, without allowing past mistakes to overshadow her self-respect. By asserting her truth and not letting the accusations define her, Casandra reclaims her place within her family while maintaining her dignity.

Both Trey and Casandra's experiences illustrate that forgiveness is a deep personal decision that does not always equate to forgetting or trusting again. Through their careful evaluations, they demonstrate that we can forgive others but must also protect ourselves from further harm by setting boundaries that align with our core values and long-term goals.

In the end, their stories remind us that forgiveness is a path to personal liberation, but accountability and self-respect are essential for protecting what matters most, whether it be a friendship, a business, or a family.

Each of these stories showcases real challenges, not just in decision-making but in navigating the complex dynamics of life, career, relationships, and personal growth. Whether it was John weighing the risks of a high-stakes investment in a startup or Amara contemplating leaving a secure job to launch her own business, these examples ask the same fundamental question: How do we balance immediate satisfaction with long-term success?

In the Win-When approach, that balance is key. It's not enough to make decisions that only provide short-term relief or gains if they come at the expense of long-term fulfillment. At the same time, making choices solely for the future, without considering how they impact your present well-being, can lead to regret, burnout, or dissatisfaction. The goal is to achieve wins that resonate both now and, in the future, decisions that align with your core values and serve you in the long run without sacrificing the present.

The Win-When Approach: A Recap of the Steps

Let's review the structured steps that guide the Win-When decision-making process:

1. Define the Decision

Every decision begins with clarity. You must clearly understand what you are deciding and why. This involves identifying the core problem or opportunity at hand. For Alyssa, it wasn't just about accepting a new job, it was about determining whether that job aligned with her deeper goals of career growth, financial security, and well-being.

2. Gather Information

The next step is information gathering. Decisions cannot be made in a vacuum. They require research, input from others, and an understanding of the broader context. Whether it's market research, talking to mentors, or seeking advice from trusted friends and colleagues, this stage helps you see all sides of the issue.

3. Weigh the Options

Once you have the necessary information, it's time to assess your choices. What are the pros and cons of each option? What are the potential rewards and the risks? Think about both the short-term and long-term consequences of your decision. Will the choice you make now support you in the future? This is where you apply critical thinking to ensure that your decision aligns with both immediate needs and future goals.

4. Align with Values and Goals

Good decisions don't just solve problems, they align with your core values. This step forces you to reflect on your personal values and long-term aspirations. Whether it's family, health, financial security, or personal fulfillment, a decision must honor those principles. For Emma, leaving her toxic relationship wasn't just about ending the conflict, it was about protecting her daughter's future and aligning with her values of safety and well-being.

5. Make the Decision

Once the options are weighed and aligned with your values, it's time to commit. This is where decisiveness comes in. You move forward, confident that you've done your homework and made a choice that will serve you now and later. This step also involves preparing for potential challenges and how you will handle them.

6. Evaluate and Adjust

Finally, no decision is set in stone. After you've made your choice, it's important to regularly evaluate its impact. Is the decision yielding the outcomes you expected? Are there adjustments you need to make along the way? This step ensures that you stay on track and that your decision remains beneficial in both the short and long term.

Role of Communication in Decision-Making

One theme that runs throughout the Win-When approach is the importance of communication. Whether you're negotiating a job offer, starting or leaving a relationship, or discussing an investment, how you communicate your decisions is crucial. Decisions don't exist in a vacuum, they often affect others, and how you share and discuss your decision can significantly influence the outcome.

Good communication involves being clear, concise, and honest. For Alyssa, setting expectations with her potential employer was key to ensuring her decision worked both for her present and future. By communicating her concerns about work-life balance, she was able to negotiate terms that aligned with her long-term goals. Similarly, Emma had to clearly communicate her decision to leave Luke, knowing it was not just about what she was saying but how she conveyed her message that would make all the difference.

In any decision-making process, you'll also need to consider how you listen to feedback. Decision-making is not a solo activity; it often involves multiple stakeholders. Whether it's a boss, a partner, a business associate, or a mentor, listening to and incorporating their input into your decision-making process can strengthen your outcome.

The Journey of Growth

As you grow into the Win-When approach, you'll notice that decision-making becomes not just a skill, but a mindset, a way of navigating life that balances immediate rewards with long-term benefits. It's a journey that encourages you to continuously refine your ability to make better decisions each day. Think of decision-making as a muscle; the more you use it with intention, the stronger and more confident you become.

Start with small decisions and apply the Win-When framework. Over time, as you become more familiar with the process, you'll find it easier to tackle bigger, more complex decisions. Whether you're contemplating a career shift, a relationship change, or a financial investment, each decision will come with greater clarity and confidence.

Remember that growth is part of the journey. You won't get everything perfect the first time. That's why the "Evaluate and Adjust" step is crucial. Don't be afraid to look back at your choices and assess what worked and what didn't. This reflection will help you evolve and make even better decisions in the future.

Incorporating the Win-When approach into your life means becoming more intentional, more thoughtful, and more aligned with your values. Every decision you make should be a stepping stone, leading you toward a future where both your present self and your future self are satisfied with the path you've chosen.

Your Next Steps:
Moving Forward with Confidence

As you close this book, I want you to leave with a sense of empowerment. The Win-When approach isn't about finding the easiest route or making a compromise. It's about discovering how to balance today's needs with tomorrow's aspirations, all while staying true to who you are.

When faced with your next decision, whether it's big or small, remember that you have the tools to navigate it thoughtfully. You've learned how to define the decision clearly, gather the right information, weigh your options, align with your values, and communicate effectively. Most importantly, you've learned that growth happens through continuous reflection and adjustment.

So, go forward with confidence. Make decisions that honor both your present and your future. And remember that with each choice, you're building a life that aligns more deeply with your values, your goals, and your highest potential. The Win-When approach is more than a method, it's a way of living that will lead you to a future filled with both immediate wins and lasting success.

Final Thoughts

As you embark on this journey of intentional decision-making, take the lessons from this book and make them your own. The Win-When approach is a flexible, dynamic way to ensure that the choices you make today set you up for success tomorrow. It's about balance, growth, and finding a way to win both in the moment and in the future.

This is your time to act. Whatever decision lies ahead of you, apply these steps, reflect deeply, and make a choice that benefits you today and tomorrow. With every decision, you're shaping the life you want to lead. So, decide wisely, communicate clearly, and most importantly, believe in your ability to win now and in the days to come.

Other Books
By Kurt Peeplez

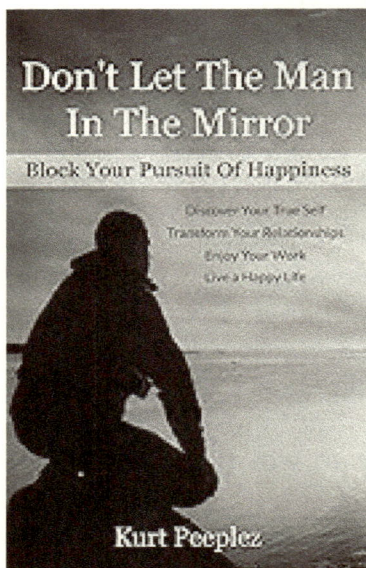

Are you struggling to feel happy and fulfilled? Do you want to break free from bad habits, and shatter old ways of thinking? Do you struggle to be honest with who you really are? Do you want to rebuild yourself as a happier individual?

Then keep reading.

Blending personal stories and insightful quotes with authentic advice and guidance, this down-to-earth book arms readers with the knowledge they need to stop sabotaging their happiness, transform their relationships, and find the strength to stay true to themselves. With practical exercises that challenge readers to take an honest look at their lives, *Don't Let the Man in the Mirror Block Your Pursuit of*

Happiness encourages you to rediscover the path to fulfillment, one small step at a time.

If you find yourself going against your better judgment just to avoid an argument, or if you stay quiet and put up with bad behavior from other people, this book offers you an actionable roadmap to **stop sacrificing your real desires** and start making yourself heard. This book explores topics of honesty, integrity, faith, and discovering your core values, so you can build an unbreakable foundation for lasting happiness.

Here's just a little of what you'll discover inside:

- The Real Reason Your Happiness Is Suffering – and What to Do About It

- Practical Steps to Improve Your Relationships and Stop Getting in Your Way

- How To Build Your Integrity, Stand Up for Your Values, and Become the Person You Want to Be

- Powerful Lessons in Faith to Help You Embrace a Strong Spiritual Center

- The Secret to Unlocking a Boundless Source of Confidence, Love, and Joy

- And So Much More...

Don't sacrifice your happiness any longer. If you're tired of ignoring your desires or compromising your true feelings, this book is an essential guide that will put you on the path to a brand-new, happier you. These tried-and-tested lessons will take you by the hand and reveal how you can heal past pain, break out of old habits, and embark on a new life philosophy.

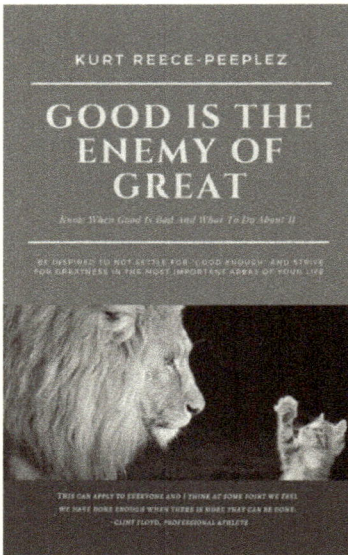

In this book, Kurt Peeplez draws on his experience as a business owner, business coach, and youth sports coach to deliver an in-depth examination of what it takes to be great and how to get there.

This easy read will inspire you to not settle for "good enough" and strive for greatness in the most important areas of your life. This book is for everyone who wants to achieve more and reach new heights.

Good can be bad if it keeps you from accomplishing something better. Many times, we allow good results to stop us from achieving something greater. If this is a regular occurrence in your life, Good is your Enemy. Read this and learn how to achieve greatness in all aspects of your life.

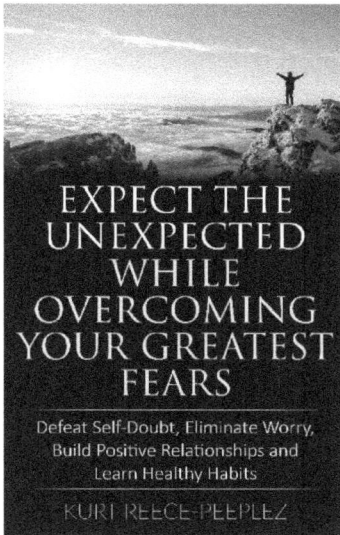

EXPECT THE UNEXPECTED WHILE OVERCOMING YOUR GREATEST FEARS

Defeat Self-Doubt, Eliminate Worry, Build Positive Relationships and Learn Healthy Habits

KURT REECE-PEEPLEZ

You'll learn to eliminate your fears within minutes of reading this book! All fear can be overcome. First, you must examine your fears and not just ride the emotion. Upon further review, you'll find that most - if not all your fears - are manageable, and you will be able to negotiate the outcomes.

I've faced many fears in my life and have found through my own experience and of those around me that we have nothing to be afraid of. When you apply knowledge and understanding to your circumstance, fear becomes an option.

This book will teach you how to turn your fears into implementable options that you can use to make your life better. Get ready to eliminate worry, defeat, and self-doubt. Learn how to build healthy habits. Enjoy this book and live your life full of options and free of fear.

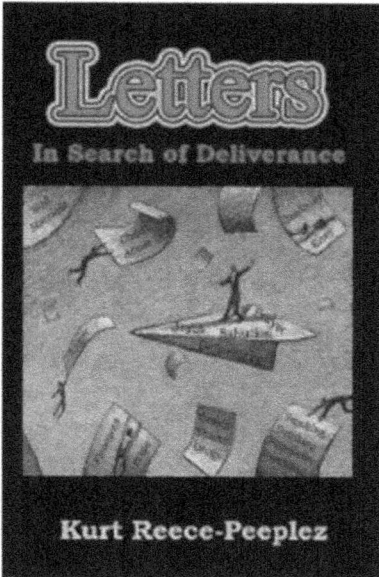

It's a fact that all need deliverance from something. No one is on the same level as God, and this is what it is all about. We are to be Holy as He is Holy, but we are imperfect.

In the book, Letters in Search of Deliverance, Author Kurt Peeplez helps us understand that we are like letters who are delivered to various places determined by how we are addressed. If it has the correct address, a letter will be delivered to the intended destination. If it has the wrong address, the letter will be delivered to the wrong place. If there is no return address, the letter may get lost or destroyed. The way you address your situations determines how successful your delivery from them will be.

Notes...